When using kitchen appliances please always follow the manufacturer's instructions.

HQ

An imprint of HarperCollins*Publishers* Ltd
1 London Bridge Street
London SE1 9GF

www.harpercollins.co.uk

HarperCollins*Publishers*
Macken House, 39/40 Mayor Street Upper,
Dublin 1, D01 C9W8, Ireland

10 9 8 7 6 5 4 3 2 1

First published in Great Britain by
HQ, an imprint of HarperCollins*Publishers* Ltd 2023

ISBN: 978-0-00-849405-6

MIX
Paper | Supporting
responsible forestry
FSC
www.fsc.org   **FSC® C007454**

This book is produced from independently certified FSC™ paper to ensure responsible forest management.

For more information visit:
www.harpercollins.co.uk/green

Photographers: Haarala Hamilton (recipe shots) and Ryan Ball (lifestyle shots)
Food styling: Elena Silcock (recipe shots) and Jessica Geddes (lifestyle shots)
Prop styling: Sarah Birks (recipe shots) and Hannah Wilkinson (lifestyle shots)
Design and Art Direction: Georgie Hewitt
Project Editor: Dan Hurst
Senior Editor: Nira Begum
Senior Production Controller: Halema Begum

Printed and bound in Italy by Rotolito S.p.A

Suzanne Mulholland

The

BATCH
LADY

COOKING ON
A BUDGET

HQ

CONTENTS

WELCOME!

The batch is back! Whoop! Another book and this time we are going BIG on saving you some of your hard-earned money.

For anyone new to the world of batching, hello! I'm Suzanne Mulholland AKA The Batch Lady and it's great to have you on board. Strap yourself in and get ready to be organised and in control of your weekly food and, perhaps most importantly, your food budget.

It has to be said that my recipes have always been designed with economy in mind, so they should never break the bank but, in this book, I've tightened up those costs further, giving you even more bang for your buck!

When I first started batch cooking it was all about saving time – as a busy working mum, I didn't want to spend every evening dashing home in a panic, wondering what I was going to feed the family. As the years went on, however, I quickly realised that another benefit of batching was that I was saving money, without even thinking about it! Gone were the days of panic buying at the expensive corner shop on my way home, or trolley dashing around the supermarket, throwing in anything that caught my eye and hoping that I had at least a few night's dinners in there before I had to repeat the process a few days later. Sound familiar?

The magic of batch cooking isn't, as many might think, just about cooking things in bulk. The magic is in being organised. By planning and preparing your meals in advance, you're investing in your future, saving yourself time and money and stopping yourself from panic impulse buying or reaching for that expensive takeaway menu.

When you cook your meals in advance, you also portion them in advance, meaning the opportunity to waste food (and the temptation to eat huge double portions just because they're there) is much lower. Cooking in this way also saves money in other areas, such as your gas and electricity bill, as well as being better for the planet – whenever I have the oven on, I'm generally cooking at least two meals, and I might also throw some baked potatoes in for the week ahead, making maximum use of the energy from the oven.

With food prices on the rise, more and more of us are finding that groceries are one of our biggest monthly spends, so why don't we treat them the same as other major purchases? If you're anything like me, you will agonise for ages over buying a new item of clothing or something for the house, asking yourself 'do I really need it?' 'Is it worth the money?' Yet, many of us hand our bank cards over at the supermarket checkout without asking these same questions because we have resigned ourselves to the fact that these foods are a necessity. But, with a little planning and a dose of batching magic, you'll be amazed at how you can hack away at those mammoth monthly bills and save yourself tons of precious time in the process.

So, whether you're part of a huge family, a new parent, a student or living alone, I really hope that this book will help take the stress out of the weekly shop and help you to get tasty meals on the table that everyone will love, whilst saving you some much-needed pennies in the process.

Believe in the batch!

HOW TO SHOP ON A BUDGET

There are some key things you can do to help reduce your food shopping bill. Some you may already know, such as not shopping when you're hungry, but others are not so obvious. Use the tips below to get yourself into the right headspace and you'll be saving pennies like a pro in no time!

MEAL PLANNING

Supermarkets are laid out with the essential items spread throughout, so you generally need to walk around the whole shop to get everything you need. With the huge range of goods on offer and special deals shouting at you from the end of the aisles, it can be hard to stay focused on what you actually need. The best way to stay on course is to make a solid plan for the week's meals before you get anywhere near the shops. Meal planning doesn't have to be set in stone and, if you want a bit of flexibility, you can plan for just five nights out of seven to factor in the occasional night out or for those days when life gets in the way and you don't have time to cook a meal.

Some people struggle knowing where to start when making a meal plan. The questions below are a great jumping-off point to get you going.

- What do you already have in the fridge/freezer/cupboard? Will any of it make a meal?
- What do you have planned for the week ahead - are there any busy nights when you'll need something quick and easy from the freezer?
- Got one meal planned? Can you double it up and make an extra meal for another night?
- Which nights during the week do you have more time to cook from scratch or double-up and make an extra meal?

Once you have the answers to all of these questions, you'll be well set to make a plan of attack for the week.

CREATE A LIST

Once you have a basic plan you can go ahead and create a shopping list of what you will need to make the plan work. Going to a store armed with a list and the determination to stick to it will help to prevent you from impulse buying.

WHERE TO SHOP

As someone who is all about saving time, I would usually advise you to stick to one shop. However, when you are on a tight budget it's good to shop around, so consider splitting your shopping between two supermarkets – one of the large supermarkets that will have everything you need combined with a smaller discount supermarket (such as Lidl or Aldi). The smaller supermarkets might not have all the brands you normally like to shop for (more on that later) but, in general, many of their basics will be cheaper. Also

consider using a supermarket that price matches, as often they have done the hard work for you. Using a points card can also help give you discounted prices on some products.

THE PROS & CONS OF ONLINE GROCERY SHOPPING

Doing a food shop online can save you money in some ways, but not in others, so it's worth trying both and seeing what one works best for you. If you do go to the shops yourself, try and remember that the products at eye level are the ones the supermarket most want you to buy and make the most profit on. Look for alternatives to the top and bottom of the shelves.

Pros

- Stops you from impulse buying
- Websites allow you to see prices per kilo, which is great when working out the best deal (especially for meat, fish etc.)
- Your login details will automatically connect to your membership or points card and show you the associated deals.
- You get a running total as you shop, so you won't get any surprises when you checkout.

Cons

- You will need to pay for delivery. Keep a look out for discounted slots, often these are when the van is already going to be in your area. Early morning and late evening slots tend to be cheaper, so can be a good option if you're watching your wallet.
- You have no control over which items get chosen for you. Some fruit and veg is sold by number of units and not weight, so, for example, a small watermelon and a large one are the same price. Buying in-store means that you can pick the best produce.
- You have no control of the sell-by dates of the products you choose. In-store you can choose the products with the longest dates.

DROP A BRAND

Dropping a brand level is an instant way to save some money. Most shops offer four product tiers: premium or luxury, branded, own-branded and value branded. Try and remember, just because something costs more it doesn't mean it's better! Often a branded product will be made in the same factory as an unbranded one, with money being saved on the labelling and marketing rather than on the product itself. If there are family favourites that you know will cause issues if you change (in my house, it's breakfast cereal!), just stick to the kind of basics that you use when you're cooking from scratch – things like tinned tomatoes, herbs, sauces, flour, canned vegetables and frozen fruit and veg. These are the things that you can change-up and save money on without anyone ever noticing the difference. Try dropping down one brand tier at a time, and if you didn't notice the difference then drop again the next time you shop for the same item. I often buy lots of value branded products for batch cooking and can genuinely say I don't notice the difference, apart from the positive impact on my wallet!

DISCOUNTED PRODUCE

Many supermarkets will discount their short-dated items a few hours before they close. This can be a good way to pick up a bargain, especially when it comes to high-priced items like meat. However, it's worth remembering that you will need to use these items quickly or get them in the freezer fast!

SIMPLE SUBSTITUTES

Over the years I've worked with fishmongers and butchers to look at ways of making simple substitutes in what we buy to save on cost. With things like meat, fish and even cheese, there are often cheaper alternatives available that taste just as good. I have added some lists below to give you some thrifty switch-ups to better-known choices.

BUDGET-FRIENDLY BEEF CUTS

Beef Shin: Great for stewing, braising or using for pulled beef

Spailbone/Featherblade: This is a great cheap cut. Ask for iron or featherblade steaks in the butcher as they offer a delicious way to enjoy a steak on a budget. Can be diced and used in stews.

Brisket: A super cheap joint of meat that is perfect for pot roasts. Cook low and slow in a pot or in a roasting dish wrapped with foil to keep it moist.

BUDGET-FRIENDLY LAMB CUTS

Shoulder: Perfect for slow cooking as a roasting joint, also works really well in a pulled lamb recipe (there's one in my first book!). It can be stuffed as well as diced for casseroles. A very versatile joint.

Minced Lamb: Great for meatballs, burgers, shepherd's pie and lamb koftas. Cheap and packed with flavour.

Lamb Shanks: Wonderful slow cooked or roasted. Make sure to cook in a pot or baking dish wrapped in foil to keep moist. Wonderful in a curry

BUDGET-FRIENDLY PORK CUTS

Pork Mince: Great for meatballs or burgers. It has a higher fat content that most mince, which works well for binding meat together.

Gammon: Delicious cooked for sandwiches, roasts etc. Can be picked up very cheaply in the supermarket and is much more economical than buying ready-cooked ham, which can be expensive.

Pork Belly: Really cheap and full of flavour. This is great slow-cooked or stuffed.

FISH

Fish that are caught on our own shores are often cheaper (and better for the planet) than the imported varieties that we are used to. Try these swaps to save money and be more sustainable.

Coley instead of **Cod**
Hake instead of **Haddock**
Trout instead of **Salmon**
Sea Cat instead of **Monkfish**
Swordfish instead of **Tuna**

CHEESE

Parma Reggiano or **Grana Padano:** much cheaper than 'proper' Parmesan, but have the same salty, umami flavour.

Greek Salad Cheese: makes a great, cheaper alternative to feta cheese.

Soft Cream Cheese: unbranded versions are much cheaper than those with recognisable brands.

FRUIT, VEG & HERBS

I'm such an advocate for frozen fruit, veg and herbs. They are generally around 20% cheaper than fresh, are frozen and packed within 30 minutes of being picked and are also peeled and chopped for you. They also keep for ages and you can use just what you need and put the rest back in the freezer, minimising food waste. What's not to love?!

If you are buying fresh fruit and veg, some supermarkets sell off boxes of 'wonky' fruit and veg at a cheaper price. These can be a great way of filling the veg drawer of your fridge for a bargain price and the produce tastes just as good as the 'perfect' stuff!

THE BENEFITS OF BATCHING

For anyone new to the world of batching you may be wondering why people batch? What are the benefits? The simple answer is that cooking this way will save you time, money, headspace and massively reduce food waste. By planning ahead and freeing up a dedicated window to prepare all of your meals for the week ahead, you are cooking when you want to, not when you have to. To a beginner, this can feel overwhelming, but give it a try and I promise you'll be amazed by how much time in the week is freed up from cooking and thinking about what to cook. A batching session is an investment in your future wellbeing, giving you more time and money to enjoy the fun stuff.

At its simplest level, cooking a double or triple batch of something often doesn't take any more time than a single batch. Take spaghetti Bolognese as an example, doubling up might lose you a couple of extra minutes browning the meat or chopping some extra veg, but that's it, and once you've finished cooking you have two or three family meals ready for the freezer that just need to be quickly defrosted and reheated later. The same applies with cost. Buying a smaller packet of minced beef is less cost effective than buying a larger one, as the price per kilo goes down when the volume goes up. Time – tick! Money – tick! That is why we batch!

GETTING STARTED

The question that I get asked the most is 'where do I start?' Relearning how you cook on a daily basis can feel like a challenge, but a few simple changes go a long way and all you really need to get started is a big pot, a tidy kitchen and some freezer bags! Then all you need to do is pick a recipe (and you're in the right place for that!).

All of the recipes in this book are designed to feed a family of four and each one includes instructions to cook from scratch to serve immediately, as well as how to prepare them for the freezer and how to reheat or cook from frozen. Once you have found a recipe that you like the look of, why not double it up and stick a portion in the freezer for a day that you don't have the time to cook from scratch? Voila! You're batching! .

THE RECIPES

As with most of my dishes, the recipes in this book are designed to be low cost and have been pared back to make sure that there are no unnecessary, pinches or dashes of ingredients that simply aren't needed. They are split into chapters on dinners, lunches and light bites, coffee house treats, desserts, fakeaways and easy entertaining, so all your needs are covered no matter how small your budget. When designing these meals I tested them all with low-cost brands to make sure they were as economical as possible, and I would encourage you to do the same to really see the pounds dropping off your shopping bill.

VEGETARIAN RECIPES

As more and more of us are looking for regular meat-free options, I wanted to include lot of vegetarian options into this book. As well as being better for the planet, eating meat-free meals a few nights a week will help cut down your food bill as, in general, these meals come in at a lower cost than meals that contain meat. If you are fully vegetarian, I have also given you more options by adding a 'Make It Veggie!' bubble to some of the recipes in this book with tips on how to convert these easily into vegetarian or vegan meals.

HALF & HALF RECIPES

Coming from a farming family that generally wants to see some form of meat in their meals, I know how tricky it can be to reduce the amount of meat that you are buying and cooking. With this in mind, I have included the option in some recipes to substitute half of the meat for extra grains or veggies. This is a great way of stretching a little bit of meat a long way, as well as getting an extra hit of veg into your family, and the best thing is that they probably won't even notice!

NO-COOK MEALS

No-cook meals are a batchers best friend as they are a great way to fill your freezer with good, tasty food in a flash! The term 'no-cook' refers to the fact that the ingredients go into the freezer raw – you simply assemble uncooked ingredients in a freezer bag, label it and put it in the freezer. It really is the work of moments. When you want to use the meal, simply take it out the freezer and follow the cooking instructions in the recipe. These are perfect for getting young kids to help in the kitchen, as they do not need to be near a hot stove. Consider assembling some of these on pay day so you know you have a stock of meals ready to go in the freezer that will see you through the rest of the month.

ZHUZH IT UP!

If you see a Zhuzh It Up! bubble on one of my recipes, this is an opportunity to add an extra bit of flair to make the end result just that little bit more special. These aren't essential and the recipes will work perfectly well without them, but they are nice options for those days when you have a few extra pennies in your purse or wallet and don't mind spending a little bit more. These are often just simple things like adding some fresh herbs for a garnish or an extra sprinkle of spice, so you can also think of your own opportunities to zhuzh based on what you already have to hand in the fridge or cupboard that needs using up.

10 MEALS
IN 1 HOUR

**Anyone who follows me on social media or who has my first book will be familiar with my
10 Meals in 1 Hour recipes. These are hour-long batching sessions that included a woven
recipe method that allows you to make 10 family meals, each feeding 4 people in the space
of a single hour. That's 40 portions of food in 60 minutes!**

In this book I have included four new menus scattered throughout the chapters. Each one focuses on a different ingredient: chicken, minced beef, tinned tuna and salmon, mushrooms, and sweet potato and butternut squash. The dishes that make up these menus can also be found elsewhere in the book as individual dishes, but these sections are brilliant if you want to fill your freezer in a flash, as the recipes have all been scaled up to feed 8 people and weaved into a single mega recipe that will leave you with 10 family meals for the freezer once you're done.

When setting up to start cooking one of these sections, I like to arrange all of the ingredients in piles by dish, then arrange them so that the ingredients for the dishes that I will be starting with are closest to me and the ones that feature later in the cooking process are further away.

It's a good idea to do a dedicated shop on the morning that you're planning on cooking one of these menus, then you can simply set everything out in the kitchen and get started. This can be a good opportunity to shop online so that when the shopping bags arrive at the door, you just need to unload them onto your kitchen sides and you're ready to go. Bear in mind that it might take you longer than an hour the first time you cook one of these menus, but you'll get quicker each time and soon enough you'll find that you're zipping through these sections in a flash - it now takes me well under an hour to get through most of them!

I've given you two full vegetarian menus in this book as those are the dishes that I often struggle for inspiration on and having a freezer full of vibrant veggie dishes ready to go takes a lot of the stress out of trying to eat meat-free meals.

The key to cooking one of these sections successfully is to start and finish with a clean kitchen. Wipe down and clear the sides before you start and clear everything down regularly as you cook. I've noted in the methods where there are natural lulls in the cooking process to do this, but just try and stay on top of it and don't worry too much about watching the clock and you'll end up with a tidy kitchen, a full freezer and the glow of knowing that you've invested one hour in saving yourself 10 meal-time's worth of cooking!

ONE JOINT, FOUR WAYS

At the back of this book you'll find a new section with recipes on how to take a single joint of meat and turn it into four delicious family meals. When researching this book it became obvious to me that one of the biggest expenses for most people in their weekly food shop is meat, so I wanted to find a way to make everyone's favourite roasts go that bit further.

When I was growing up there wasn't a lot of spare cash in the house, so my family would often make a whole roast chicken or joint of beef stretch over several meals. Buying a whole chicken in this way is so much more economical than purchasing ready portioned chicken breasts, which work out around three times the cost when you look at the price per kilo!

The menus that I have included at the back of the book (pages 228–247) include chicken, beef brisket and gammon and will show you how to really get the most out of your meat and use every last morsel. These are different from the 10 Meals in 1 Hour Sections in that they do take a bit more time, but you can get started with some prep while your joint of meat is roasting.

One of the things that I love about these sections is that they show how meat doesn't have to be the star of a meal – it can also be the side-kick! A little bit of succulent meat can really lift a dish and will keep the carnivores at your table happy, but you only need a little to make a dish feel special. If you take a roast dinner for example, it is often the roast potatoes, Yorkshire puddings or cauliflower cheese that are the real stars of the show, with the meat acting as the support act.

The sizes of meat and the suggested cooking times are all guidelines. If you can't get the exact size that I suggest then buy a slightly bigger joint and adjust the cooking times accordingly –if you're buying a packaged joint from supermarket it will likely include a suggested cooking time. As with the other recipes in this book, these dishes are designed to be made ahead and stored in the freezer. Because of this it's important that you're only using fresh meat that hasn't been defrosted or frozen already. That way, you can happily freeze the meat after it is cooked without worrying.

If you're going to be carving thin slivers of meat or chopping it up into chunks, it's important that you have a sharp, good-quality carving knife. A blunt knife will slow you down and make precision carving difficult. Having a good knife can mean the difference between getting 30 thin slices of meat versus 10 thick ones, so it really is worth ensuring that you have one to hand.

Each menu includes a roast dinner, because if your family is anything like mine then this will be a staple! But I've left the sides up to you, so supplement with roast potatoes, Yorkshire puddings and all those other good things as needed.

As with the 10 Meals in 1 Hour sections, the key to success with these menus is preparation! Start with a clean kitchen and arrange all of your ingredients in piles according to the order you are cooking the dishes. I tend to get my joints in the oven first then use the time they are cooking to prepare my other ingredients.

COOKING, FREEZING & DEFROSTING

Every recipe in this book can be cooked fresh or made in advance and stored in the freezer until needed and, as with my previous books, every recipe contains instructions on how to do both. Simply follow the method, then when you get to the end of the numbered steps either continue down the page to cook now or jump to the bottom for instructions on freezing and reheating. There are handy headings to make it as clear and easy to follow as possible, but it's worth familiarising yourself with the style of my recipe methods before you start to cook your first meal.

HOW TO FREEZE MEALS

Use the guidelines below to get to grips with the simplest and safest way of preparing your meals for the freezer.

- Set any cooked meals aside to cool down to room temperature before sealing them and adding to the freezer.
- If you are making a no-cook meal (see page 16) that contains ready-frozen vegetables, work fast and get these in the freezer as soon as you have made them to avoid the veg defrosting.
- Remember to clearly label all freezer bags with the name of the meal, how many it caters for, the date it was made and any cooking instructions. Many

meals look the same when frozen, so this can save you from the perils of the UFO (unidentified frozen object)!

- Where possible, freeze meals in bags, expelling any air and lying flat so that you can stack them on top of one another and make the most efficient use of the space in your freezer. Freezing meals in this way also helps them to defrost quickly.
- If you are freezing multiple meals at a time, space them out around your freezer rather than stacking them on top of each other. Surrounding unfrozen meals with frozen meals will help them to freeze quicker and preserve the quality of the food.

THE THREE DEFROSTING METHODS

When it comes to defrosting a meal for the next day, I set a reoccurring daily alarm on my phone to go off at dinner time, so I remember to take the next night's meal out the freezer. You will be in the kitchen anyway, so it becomes a two-minute job. Once your meal is out of the freezer, you can defrost it in one of three ways:

IN THE FRIDGE

If the recipe says to defrost before cooking, you can place in the fridge overnight and it will be defrosted by the next day. Remember to always add a drip tray or dish under your defrosting meal to catch any water that collects as the meal defrosts.

THE WATER METHOD

This is my favourite method of defrosting, as it's really fast and can be used if you have forgotten to take something out of the freezer the night before. Make sure the bag or container that your food is in is airtight, then place it in a basin of cold water (never hot!).

Within 20 minutes the meal should be on its way to defrosting. This method is great if you have meals that are frozen flat in bags (see page 22), as they are so thin they will defrost rapidly.

IN THE MICROWAVE

Most microwaves have dedicated defrosting programmes. Simply follow the manufacturer's

guidelines for your specific model, remembering to stir your food part way through the defrost cycle.

COOKING FROM FROZEN

I adore meals that can be cooked from frozen. Remove a meal from the freezer, put it in the oven and your work is done! The list below contains all the meals in

this book that can be cooked from frozen – see the individual recipes for cooking instructions. All reheated meals should reach 74°C/165°F before serving.

DISHES THAT CAN BE COOKED FROM FROZEN

Veggie

- Breaded Halloumi Fries (p.140)
- Cauliflower & Chickpea Madras (p.132)
- Easy Falafels (p.49)
- Garlicky Breaded Mushrooms (p.58)
- Low-Cost Lentil Soup (p.37)
- Mushroom Bolognese (p.98)
- Pasta Arrabiata Sauce (p.62)
- Thai Sweet Potato Soup (p.38)
- Veggie Empanadas (p.51)
- Veggie Stew & Herb Dumplings (p.108)

Meat

- Beef Empanadas (p.50)
- Beef Keema (p.134)
- BFC Chicken (p.138)
- Butter Chicken (p.128)
- Cheeseburger Sausage Roll (p.41)
- Chicken & Vegetable Fricassee (p.72)
- Chicken Dhansak (p.129)
- Croque Monsieur (p.44)
- Half & Half Lentil Bolognese (p.77)
- Ham & Cheese Croquette Cakes (p.55)
- Meatball Toad in the Hole (p.96)
- Mexican Beef Pasta Bake (p.81)

Sweet Treats

- Apple and Cinnamon Crumble (p.210)
- Churros (p.222)
- Cinnamon Swirls (p.194)

BATCHING KIT LIST

You don't need lots of expensive kit to start batching, but there are some key items that will definitely make things a little easier. The list below is what I use regularly, but if you're just starting out you can build up your kit as you become more confident and experienced.

MEASURING CUPS

Throughout this book, you'll notice that I give both cup and gram measurements for my ingredients, this is because spooning in a cup of an ingredients is far quicker than weighing it out – and batching is all about saving time! I like to use spoon-shaped measuring cups, as these can also be used for stirring dishes and portion control. It's important to realise that a measuring cup is a set size, so using any mug from the cupboard won't cut it! For reference, I have listed cup sizes and their equivalents in millilitres and tablespoons below.

CUP MEASUREMENTS

1 cup = 240ml = 16 tablespoons

¾ cup = 180ml = 12 tablespoons

⅔ cup = 160ml = 11 tablespoons

½ cup = 120ml = 8 tablespoons

⅓ cup = 80ml = 5½ tablespoons

¼ cup = 60 ml = 4 tablespoons

PORTIONING OUT WITH CUPS

If you're on a budget then you want to make sure you portion out meals correctly to get the right amount of servings per recipe and stretch them as far as possible. If you have doubled a recipe or completed a 10 meals in 1 hour section, then it can be hard to know how many portions you have in your pot. As a rule, one cup of scoopable food (curry, stew, Bolognese) is one adult portion. For children under 10, half a cup is a portion.

LARGE NON-STICK POTS

These can be bought relatively inexpensively at supermarkets and make the perfect cooking vessel for large batches of the kind of meal that needs to bubble away on the stove. If possible, get two pots so that you can make the most of your batching time and have multiple meals on the go. Try to get stainless steel pots with heatproof handles that can be transferred to the oven if needed.

FREEZER BAGS

You can get sealable plastic bags in a variety of sizes at your local supermarket. These can be washed and reused several times before throwing away, which will save money and is also better for the environment. Biodegradable bags are available too, though these are sadly more expensive. PEVA bags are reusable freezer bags that can be used up to 300 times before being thrown away, but these are an investment, so I suggest building up a collection gradually until you have a good stock. These bags need to be washed out after use, but you can't put hot food in them or put them in the dishwasher.

MARKERS AND CHALK PENS

Labelling your meals is a must! You only need one good pen, just make sure to hide it in a safe place so only you know where it is! Permanent marker pens work well on plastic freezer bags but do not wash off, chalk pens are my preference as the writing stays on when in the freezer but is easily washed off with hot soapy water, allowing you to reuse the bag or tub again. **Top Tip:** Filled bags do not label well, so always label your bag before filling.

FREEZER-TO-OVEN BAKING DISHES

These are glass dishes with plastic lids that will happily go straight from the freezer to the oven. They are great for recipes like lasagne or enchiladas when a bag simply won't do the job. Keep an eye out for bargains as these are often heavily discounted in large supermarkets and homeware stores.

THE RECIPES

LIGHT BITES & LUNCHES

CHICKEN & MUSHROOM RAMEN

This recipe serves four but I like to freeze it in individual portions so that it can easily be grabbed from the freezer for an easy solo meal. It would make a great option for a work lunch, as all you need to do is add boiling water at the office for something much more exciting (and kinder on the wallet) than a sandwich from the local supermarket!

PREP: 10 MINS
COOK: 12–14 MINS
SERVES: 4

1 tbsp sesame or vegetable oil
1 tbsp frozen chopped garlic
1 tbsp frozen chopped ginger
2 skinless, boneless chicken breasts, thinly sliced
8 white mushrooms, sliced
1 carrot, peeled and grated
1 tbsp soy sauce
2 chicken stock cubes
2 tbsp chopped chives
4 blocks dried chicken noodles
4 eggs, to serve (optional)

1 Heat the oil in a large, deep-sided frying pan over a medium heat, then add the garlic and ginger and cook, stirring, for 2 minutes, until soft and fragrant.
2 Add the sliced chicken to the pan and cook, stirring continuously, for 2–3 minutes, until well-sealed and coated in the garlic and ginger.
3 Add the mushrooms, carrot and soy sauce to the pan and cook for a further 2 minutes, until the veg are just starting to soften.

IF YOU'RE MAKING AHEAD TO *Freeze*...**SKIP TO THE BOTTOM**

IF YOU'RE COOKING *Now*... Dissolve the stock cubes in 8 cups (2 litres) of boiling water, then add to the pan along with the chives and the dried noodles. Bring to the boil, then reduce the heat to a gentle simmer and leave to cook for 6 minutes.

Meanwhile, if you are serving the ramen with boiled eggs, bring a separate pan of water to the boil and cook the eggs for 7 minutes, then immediately drain and rinse under cold running water to stop the eggs from cooking further (this should give you eggs that are firm enough to peel, with yolks that are still slightly soft and jammy). Peel the eggs and cut into halves. Divide the noodles, veg and broth between 4 serving bowls, then add half a boiled egg to each bowl. Serve hot.

IF YOU'RE MAKING AHEAD TO *Freeze*...
Remove the pan from the heat and set aside until the vegetables have cooled to room temperature, then divide the mixture equally between 4 small, labelled freezer bags. Grate half a stock cube into each bag along with 1 block of dried noodles and half a tablespoon of chives, then seal and freeze flat for up to 3 months.

Then... Remove as many portions of ramen mixture as you would like from the freezer and add to a large bowl (use an individual serving bowl if you are defrosting a single portion). Pour over 2 cups (480ml) of boiling water for each portion of ramen you have defrosted, then cook on high in the microwave for 8 minutes, stirring the mixture halfway through. If you want to serve the ramen with the boiled eggs, cook these as described above whilst the ramen mixture is cooking in the microwave. Divide the mixture between serving bowls, top each with half a boiled egg, if using, then serve hot.

CREAMY MUSHROOM SOUP

This rich, earthy soup makes the perfect lunch or light meal on chilly autumnal days when you are craving something warming, or would equally make a lovely starter at a dinner party. This also features in my menu for 10 Mushroom Meals in 1 Hour (pages 120–125), so if you enjoy it then try cooking through the whole menu to fill your freezer with mushroomy goodness.

PREP: 5 MINS
COOK: 15 MINS
SERVES: 4

1 tbsp olive or vegetable oil
2 cups (230g) frozen chopped
  onions
2 tsp frozen chopped garlic
625g white mushrooms, sliced
4 cups (970ml) vegetable stock
1 tbsp frozen chopped parsley
½ cup (120ml) double cream
salt and freshly ground black pepper
crusty bread and butter, to serve
  (optional)

1 Heat the oil in a large pan over a medium heat. Add the onions, garlic and mushrooms and cook, stirring, for a couple of minutes, until the vegetables are soft.
2 Add the vegetable stock, parsley and a generous grinding of salt and pepper, bring the mixture to a boil, then reduce to a gentle simmer and leave to cook for 15 minutes, stirring occasionally.
3 Remove the pan from the heat and stir in the cream, then use a stick blender to blend the soup until smooth.

IF YOU'RE MAKING AHEAD TO *Freeze*...**SKIP TO THE BOTTOM**

IF YOU'RE SERVING *Now*... Simply ladle the soup into serving bowls and serve hot, with crusty bread and butter on the side for dunking, if you like.

Zhuzh it up...
Dress the soup with a swirl of double cream and a sprinkling of freshly chopped parsley.

IF YOU'RE MAKING AHEAD TO *Freeze*...
Set the soup aside to cool to room temperature, then transfer to a large, labelled freezer bag (a soup or sauce bag is perfect for this) and freeze flat for up to 3 months.

Then... Remove the soup from the freezer and place it in the fridge to defrost. Once defrosted, pour the soup into a large pan and place over medium-low heat until piping hot all of the way through.

LOW-COST LENTIL SOUP

Lentils are cheap, packed with goodness and will sit happily in the cupboard until needed, so are a brilliant ingredient to stock up on. This lentil soup makes a hearty lunch or simple supper and, when packed in a flask, makes a wonderful on-the-go meal to warm you up at work or sustain you on a winter walk.

PREP: 5 MINS
COOK: 45 MINS
SERVES: 4

1 tbsp olive or vegetable oil
1 cup (115g) frozen chopped onions
2 tsp frozen chopped garlic
4 stalks celery, finely chopped
3 large carrots, peeled and finely chopped
¾ cup (150g) red lentils
8 cups (2 litres) vegetable stock
salt and freshly ground black pepper
crusty bread and butter, to serve (optional)

1 Heat the oil in a large pan over a medium heat. Add the onions, garlic, celery and carrots, and cook, stirring, for 2–3 minutes, until starting to soften

2 Add the lentils to the pan along with a generous grinding of salt and pepper and stir to combine. Pour in the stock, bring the soup to the boil, then reduce to a simmer and leave to cook, loosely covered, for around 45 minutes, until the lentils are tender.

3 Remove the pan from the heat. If you prefer a smooth soup, use a stick blender to blend until smooth.

IF YOU'RE MAKING AHEAD TO *Freeze*...**SKIP TO THE BOTTOM**

IF YOU'RE SERVING *Now*... Simply ladle the soup into serving bowls and serve hot, with crusty bread and butter on the side for dunking, if you like.

Zhuzh it up...
Fry a few bacon rashers until crisp, then snip these over the surface of the soup before serving.

IF YOU'RE MAKING AHEAD TO
Freeze... Set the soup aside to cool to room temperature, then transfer to a large, labelled freezer bag (a soup or sauce bag is perfect for this) and freeze flat for up to 3 months.

Then... This can be reheated from defrosted or while frozen. If defrosting first, remove the soup from the freezer and place it in the fridge to defrost. Once defrosted, pour the soup into a large pan and place over a medium-low heat until piping hot all of the way through. If heating from frozen, put the frozen soup in a pan over a low heat and warm gently, breaking up the soup with a wooden spoon as you do, until fully melted and piping hot all of the way through.

THAI SWEET POTATO SOUP

This Thai-style soup is sure to brighten up the dullest of days with its vibrant colour and warming punch of spice. It's got a bit of kick to it, so use a little less of the curry paste if you prefer milder flavours.

PREP: 10 MINS
COOK: 30 MINS
SERVES: 4

1 tbsp olive or vegetable oil
1 cup (115g) frozen chopped onions
2 tsp frozen chopped garlic
1 tsp frozen chopped ginger
2–3 tbsp Thai green curry paste
1 cup (175g) frozen sliced peppers
500g bag frozen sweet potato
  chunks
1 x 400g tin coconut milk
3 cups (720ml) vegetable stock
juice of 1 lime
2 tsp frozen chopped coriander
salt and freshly ground black pepper
crusty bread and butter, to serve
  (optional)

1 Heat the oil in a large pan over a medium heat. Add the onions, garlic and ginger, and cook, stirring, for 2–3 minutes, until soft.
2 Add the curry paste to the pan and stir to combine with the onions, then add the peppers, sweet potato chunks, coconut milk and vegetable stock and stir again.
3 Bring the soup to the boil, then reduce to a gentle simmer and leave to cook, covered, for 30 minutes, until all of the vegetables are tender.
4 Remove the pan from the heat, then use a stick blender to blend the soup until smooth. Season generously with salt and pepper, then stir through the lime juice and coriander.

IF YOU'RE MAKING AHEAD TO *Freeze*...**SKIP TO THE BOTTOM**

IF YOU'RE SERVING *Now*... Simply ladle the soup into serving bowls and serve hot, with crusty bread and butter on the side for dunking, if you like.

IF YOU'RE MAKING AHEAD TO *Freeze*...
Set the soup aside to cool to room temperature, then transfer to a large, labelled freezer bag (a soup or sauce bag is perfect for this) and freeze flat for up to 3 months.

Then... This can be reheated from defrosted or while frozen. If defrosting first, remove the soup from the freezer and place it in the fridge to defrost. Once defrosted, pour the soup into a large pan and place over a medium-low heat until piping hot all of the way through. If heating from frozen, put the frozen soup in a pan with a little water over a low heat and warm gently, breaking up the soup with a wooden spoon as you do, until fully melted and piping hot all of the way through.

CHEESEBURGER SAUSAGE ROLL

This recipe fuses two family favourites – a cheeseburger and a sausage roll – in one delicious package! It makes a great grab-and-go lunch, but you could also dress it up with salad and chips or wedges for a more substantial meal.

PREP: 10 MINS
COOK: 40 MINS
SERVES: 4

2 eggs
500g minced beef
2 tbsp Worcestershire sauce
1 tbsp American mustard
1 sheet pre-rolled puff pastry
1 cup (90g) pre-grated Cheddar cheese
2 tbsp tomato ketchup
salt and freshly ground black pepper

1. Beat one of the eggs into a large mixing bowl and add the minced beef, Worcestershire sauce, mustard and a generous grinding each of salt and pepper. Using your hands, combine the mixture until well incorporated.
2. Unroll the puff pastry, keeping it on its baking paper lining, and set it on the work surface so that the wider edges are at the top and bottom. Using a sharp knife, score a horizontal line through the middle of the pastry to divide it into 2 halves, being sure not to cut all the way through.
3. Leaving a 2.5cm (1 inch) border around the edge of the pastry, spoon the beef mixture into the centre of the top half of the pastry sheet and form it into an even sausage shape with your hands, then sprinkle the grated Cheddar over the top in an even layer.
4. Leaving a 2.5cm (1 inch) border around the edge, evenly spread the tomato ketchup over the bottom half of the pastry sheet.
5. Crack the remaining egg into a small bowl and beat to combine, then brush the border around the sheet of pastry with the egg wash.
6. Bring the bottom half of the pastry up and over the top half to encase the beef sausage in the pastry, then use a fork to press all around the edges of the pastry to seal.

IF YOU'RE MAKING AHEAD TO *Freeze*...SKIP TO THE BOTTOM

IF YOU'RE COOKING *Now*... Transfer the sausage roll, still on its baking paper, to a large baking sheet and brush the top and sides with the remaining egg wash. Transfer to an oven preheated to 180°C/350°F/gas mark 4 and leave to bake for 40 minutes, until golden. Cut the sausage roll into 4 equal-sized pieces and serve with salad, chips and lashings of ketchup and mustard on the side, if you like.

IF YOU'RE MAKING AHEAD TO *Freeze*...
Wrap the uncooked sausage roll up tightly in its baking paper wrapper, then wrap again in a couple of layers of clingfilm. Label clearly and freeze for up to 3 months.

Then... This can be cooked from frozen or defrosted first. To cook from frozen, unwrap the sausage roll, place on a lined baking sheet and brush the top and sides with a little egg wash. Transfer to an oven preheated to 180°C/350°F/gas mark 4 and leave to bake for 1 hour, until golden, covering the sausage roll with foil if it starts to catch. To cook from defrosted, leave the sausage roll in the fridge to defrost, then cook in the same way, reducing the cooking time to 40 minutes.

SQUASH, BEETROOT & GOATS CHEESE PUFF ROLL

PREP: 10 MINS
COOK: 65–70 MINS
SERVES: 4

1 x 500g bag frozen butternut
  squash chunks
2 tbsp olive or vegetable oil
2 tsp dried thyme
250g cooked whole beetroot
150g soft goats' cheese, crumbled
1 sheet pre-rolled puff pastry
2 tbsp pesto
1 egg, beaten
salad, to serve (optional)

1   Preheat the oven to 180°C/350°F/gas mark 4 and line a baking sheet with foil. Spread the sweet potato chunks over the baking sheet, then drizzle with the olive oil and sprinkle over the thyme. Transfer to the oven for 25–30 minutes, until tender and just golden. Set aside to cool.

3   While the squash is cooling, drain the beetroot and cut each ball into 8 slices. Put the beetroot slices in a large bowl along with the crumbled goats' cheese and the cooled butternut squash. Mix well to combine.

4   Unroll the puff pastry, keeping it on its baking paper lining, and set it on the work surface so that the wider edges are at the top and bottom. Using a sharp knife, lightly score a horizontal line through the middle of the pastry to divide it into 2 halves, being sure not to cut all the way through.

5   Leaving a 2.5cm (1 inch) border around the edge of the pastry, spoon the squash and beetroot mixture into the centre of the top half of the pastry sheet and form it into an even rectangular shape with your hands.

6   Leaving a 2.5cm (1 inch) border around the edge, evenly spread the pesto over the bottom half of the pastry sheet.

7   Brush the border around the sheet of pastry with the beaten egg, then bring the bottom half of the pastry up and over the top half to encase the filling. Use a fork to press all around the edges of the pastry to seal.

IF YOU'RE MAKING AHEAD TO *Freeze*...**SKIP TO THE BOTTOM**

IF YOU'RE COOKING *Now*... Transfer the puff roll, still on its baking paper, to a large baking sheet and brush the top and sides with the remaining egg wash. Transfer to an oven preheated to 180°C/350°F/gas mark 4 and leave to bake for 40 minutes, until golden. Cut the roll into 4 equal-sized pieces and serve with salad alongside, if you like.

IF YOU'RE MAKING AHEAD TO *Freeze*...
Wrap the uncooked puff roll up tightly in its baking paper wrapper, then wrap again in a couple of layers of clingfilm. Label clearly and freeze for up to 3 months.

Then... This can be cooked from frozen or defrosted first. To cook from frozen, simply unwrap the puff roll, place on a baking paper-lined baking sheet and brush the top and sides with a little egg wash. Transfer to an oven preheated to 180°C/350°F/gas mark 4 and leave to bake for 1 hour, until golden, covering with foil if it starts to catch. To cook from defrosted, put the puff roll in the fridge overnight and allow to defrost, then cook in the same way, but reducing the cooking time to 40 minutes.

CROQUE MONSIEUR

This is the ultimate cheese and ham toastie. They freeze brilliantly and can be reheated straight from frozen, so get them in the freezer for a rainy day when you are craving something overflowing with golden, bubbling cheesy deliciousness!

PREP: 10 MINS
COOK: 12–15 MINS
SERVES: 4

8 slices white bread
3 tbsp butter
3 tbsp plain flour
1⅓ cups (320ml) milk
4 tsp Dijon mustard
8 slices Emmental cheese
4 slices ham
2 cups (180g) pre-grated Cheddar cheese
salt and freshly ground black pepper
salad, to serve (optional)

MAKE IT Veggie!

Simply swap to plant-based ham for a vegetarian version of this classic.

1　Preheat the grill to high and line a large baking sheet with foil.

2　Lay the bread on the baking sheet and toast under the grill until just golden on the top sides. Remove from the grill and set aside to cool.

3　Melt the butter in a small pan over a medium heat, then add the flour and whisk to a thick paste. Gradually add the milk, whisking and thickening the sauce between each addition, until it is all used up and you have a thick, glossy sauce. Cook for 2 minutes, then season generously, remove from the heat and set aside.

4　Set 4 slices of the bread in front of you on the baking sheet, toasted sides up, and spread each with 1 teaspoon of Dijon mustard. Top each piece of bread with 2 slices of Emmental cheese, followed by 1 slice of ham.

5　Spread each of the untoasted sides of the 4 remaining pieces of bread with a heaped tablespoon of white sauce, then used these to sandwich the other pieces of bread, sauce-side down. Spread the tops of the sandwiches with the remaining white sauce.

IF YOU'RE MAKING AHEAD TO *Freeze*...SKIP TO THE BOTTOM

IF YOU'RE COOKING *Now*... Top each sandwich with a small handful (around ½ cup/45g) of grated Cheddar. Put the baking sheet with the sandwiches under a preheated grill and cook for 5–10 minutes, until golden, bubbling and piping hot all of the way through. Serve hot with salad alongside, if you like.

IF YOU'RE MAKING AHEAD TO *Freeze*... Put the baking sheet with the uncooked sandwiches in the freezer for 1 hour to flash-freeze, then transfer the sandwiches to a large, labelled freezer bag and freeze flat for up to 3 months.

Then... These are best cooked straight from frozen. Simply lay the frozen sandwiches on a foil-lined baking sheet, top each with a small handful (around ½ cup/45g) of grated Cheddar and place under a preheated grill for 8–10 minutes, until golden, bubbling and piping hot all of the way through.

TUNA MELT PANINIS

This is a homemade version of those £5 cafe paninis, but at a fraction of the cost. I like to have a stash of these in the freezer ready to cook when I hear the call of the coffee shop – they more than satisfy the craving and save me a lot of money in the process. These paninis also feature in the 10 Meals in 1 Hour menu on pages 164–169.

PREP: 10 MINS
COOK: 5–10 MINS
SERVES: 4

2 x 145g cans tuna, drained
½ red onion, finely chopped
2 heaped tbsp mayonnaise
4 panini rolls
2 cups (180g) pre-grated Cheddar cheese
salt and freshly ground black pepper
salad and crisps, to serve (optional)

1   Flake the tuna into a bowl, then add the red onion and mayonnaise and mix to combine.
2   Slice open the panini rolls and spread one half of each roll with the tuna and onion mixture.
3   Top the tuna-spread half of each panini roll with a handful (around ½ cup/90g) of grated Cheddar, then sandwich the rolls with the untopped halves of the rolls.

IF YOU'RE MAKING AHEAD TO *Freeze*...**SKIP TO THE BOTTOM**

IF YOU'RE COOKING *Now*... Preheat a panini maker, then toast the paninis for 5–6 minutes until the paninis are crisp and the cheese is melted and bubbling. Serve the paninis with salad and crisps on the side, if you like.

IF YOU'RE MAKING AHEAD TO *Freeze*...
Wrap each of the uncooked paninis in foil, then transfer to a large, labelled freezer bag and freeze flat for up to 3 months.

Then... Remove individual paninis from the freezer as needed. Unwrap the foil, then place in the microwave on defrost for 2 minutes. Once defrosted, toast in a preheated panini maker for 4 minutes, until the bread is crisp and the cheese is melted and bubbling

EASY FALAFELS

These are healthy, delicious and can be cooked straight from frozen, so are great for grabbing from the freezer straight into the oven for a quick and easy lunch. I like to serve mine in toasted pitta breads with salad, feta cheese and a drizzle of chilli sauce.

PREP: 5–10 MINS
COOK: 20–25 MINS
SERVES: 4

2 x 400g cans chickpeas, drained
2 tsp frozen chopped garlic
1 cup (115g) frozen chopped onions
2 tsp ground coriander
2 tsp ground cumin
large handful fresh coriander, finely
  chopped
large handful fresh parsley, finely
  chopped
3 tbsp plain flour
1 tsp salt
freshly ground black pepper

To serve:
hummus, pitta breads, chilli sauce
  and crumbled feta cheese
  (optional)

1 Put all of the falafel ingredients and a generous grinding of black pepper in a food processor and blitz until everything is well combined and the mixture has come together into a ball. If you don't have a food processor, you can also do this with a stick blender, though you may need to add a splash of water to help the mixture to start to blend.
2 Roll the mixture into 12 equal balls with your hands, then flatten them slightly into disc shapes.

IF YOU'RE MAKING AHEAD TO *Freeze*...SKIP TO THE BOTTOM

IF YOU'RE COOKING *Now*... Lay the falafel on a foil-lined baking sheet and drizzle over a little oil. Transfer to an oven preheated to 180°C/350°F/gas mark 4 and bake for 20–25 minutes, until crisp and golden. Serve hot, stuffed into toasted pitta breads with hummus and crumbled feta cheese, if you like.

IF YOU'RE MAKING AHEAD TO *Freeze*... Lay the falafel on a foil-lined baking sheet, then transfer the entire baking sheet to the freezer for 1 hour to flash-freeze. After an hour, transfer the frozen falafel to a large, labelled freezer bag and freeze flat for up to 3 months.

***Then*...** These can be cooked straight from frozen. Lay the falafel on a foil-lined baking sheet and drizzle over a little oil. Transfer to an oven preheated to 180°C/350°F/gas mark 4 and bake for 25–30 minutes, until crisp and golden.

BEEF EMPANADAS

PREP: 15 MINS
COOK: 40-45 MINS
MAKES: 16-18 empanadas

1 small sweet potato (around
   200g), peeled and cut into 1cm/½
   inch chunks
1 tbsp olive or vegetable oil
½ red onion, finely chopped
2 tsp frozen chopped garlic
250g minced beef
2 tbsp tomato purée
1 tsp ground cumin
1 tsp smoked paprika
2 spring onions, finely sliced
juice of 1 lime
2 sheets pre-rolled shortcrust
   pastry
1 egg, beaten
salt and freshly ground black pepper

1 Preheat the oven to 180°C/350°F/gas mark 4. Line a baking sheet with foil and spread the sweet potato chunks over, then transfer to the oven and cook for 20–25 minutes, until tender.

2 Meanwhile, heat the oil in a frying pan over a medium heat, then add the onion and garlic and cook for 2–3 minutes, stirring, until soft.

3 Add the beef to the pan and cook, breaking it up with a wooden spoon, for 8–10 minutes, until browned.

4 Add the tomato purée, ground cumin, paprika, a generous grinding of salt and pepper and a splash of water to the pan and continue to cook for 2–3 minutes to allow the spices to meld. Remove from the heat, stir through the spring onions, cooked sweet potato chunks and lime juice, then set aside to cool to room temperature.

5 While the filling is cooling, unroll the sheets of pastry on their paper backing and stamp out 10cm/4 inch rounds with a pastry cutter. Once you have stamped out as many rounds as possible, reroll the pastry scraps and stamp out as many more rounds as you can.

6 Put a tablespoon of filling in the centre of each round of pastry, brush round the edges with a little beaten egg, then bring the bottom edge of each pastry round up and over the filling to enclose it in a neat semi-circle shape. Press around the edges with a fork to seal, then brush the top of each empanada with a little more beaten egg.

IF YOU'RE MAKING AHEAD TO *Freeze*...SKIP TO THE BOTTOM

IF YOU'RE COOKING *Now*... Lay the empanadas on a foil-lined baking sheet and transfer to an oven preheated to 180°C/350°F/gas mark 4 to bake for 20 minutes, until golden. Serve 3–4 empanadas per person.

IF YOU'RE MAKING AHEAD TO *Freeze*... You can either freeze the empanadas cooked or uncooked. If freezing from uncooked, lay the empanadas on a foil-lined baking sheet and put the whole tray in the freezer to flash freeze for 1 hour, then transfer to a large, labelled freezer bag and freeze for up to 3 months. If freezing from cooked, simply cook as described above, leave the cooked empanadas to cool to room temperature, then transfer to a large, labelled freezer bag and freeze for up to 3 months.

Then... If they weren't cooked before freezing, lay the frozen empanadas on a foil-lined baking sheet and transfer to an oven preheated to 180°C/350°F/gas mark 4 and bake for 30–35 minutes, until golden and piping hot all of the way through. If they were frozen already cooked, reduce the cooking time to 10 minutes, making sure the empanadas are piping hot all of the way through before serving.

VEGGIE EMPANADAS

PREP: 20 MINS
COOK: 40–45 MINS
MAKES: 16–18 empanadas

1 small sweet potato (around 200g), peeled and cut into 2cm/1 inch chunks
1 cup (120g) frozen sweetcorn
1 tsp ground cumin
1 tsp smoked paprika
1 x 400g can black beans, drained
2 spring onions, finely sliced
juice of 1 lime
1 cup (90g) pre-grated Cheddar cheese
1 tbsp frozen chopped coriander
2 sheets pre-rolled shortcrust pastry
1 egg, beaten
salt and freshly ground black pepper

1 Preheat the oven to 180°C/350°F/gas mark 4. Line a baking sheet with foil and spread the sweet potato chunks over, then transfer to the oven and cook for 20–25 minutes, until tender and golden.

2 Remove the sweet potato from the oven and add the sweetcorn, ground cumin, paprika and black beans to the baking sheet and give everything a stir to coat the veg in the spices. Return the tray to the oven and cook for another 8 minutes, until everything is cooked through, then set aside to cool to room temperature.

3 Once cooled, transfer the cooked vegetable mixture to a large bowl and add the spring onions, lime juice, grated Cheddar and frozen coriander and mix well to combine.

4 Unroll the sheets of pastry on their paper backing and stamp out 10cm/4 inch rounds with a pastry cutter. Once you have stamped out as many rounds as possible, re-roll the pastry scraps and stamp out as many more rounds as you can.

5 Put a tablespoon of filling in the centre of each round of pastry, brush round the edges with a little beaten egg, then bring the bottom edge of each pastry round up and over the filling to enclose it in a neat semi-circle shape. Press around the edges with a fork to seal. Brush the top of each empanada with a little more beaten egg.

IF YOU'RE MAKING AHEAD TO *Freeze*...SKIP TO THE BOTTOM

IF YOU'RE COOKING *Now*... Lay the empanadas on a foil-lined baking sheet and transfer to an oven preheated to 180°C/350°F/gas mark 4 to bake for 20 minutes, until golden. Serve 3–4 empanadas per person.

IF YOU'RE MAKING AHEAD TO *Freeze*... You can either freeze the empanadas cooked or uncooked. If freezing from uncooked, lay the empanadas on a foil-lined baking sheet and put the whole tray in the freezer to flash freeze for 1 hour, then transfer to a large, labelled freezer bag and freeze for up to 3 months. If freezing from cooked, simply cook as described above, leave the cooked empanadas to cool to room temperature, then transfer to a large, labelled freezer bag and freeze for up to 3 months.

Then... If they weren't cooked before freezing, lay the frozen empanadas on a foil-lined baking sheet and transfer to an oven preheated to 180°C/350°F/gas mark 4 and bake for 30–35 minutes, until golden and piping hot all of the way through. If they were frozen already cooked, reduce the cooking time to 10 minutes, making sure the empanadas are piping hot all of the way through before serving. Alternatively, reheat them from frozen in the microwave for 1½ minutes, until piping hot all the way through.

HAM & CHEESE CROQUETTE CAKES

These crunchy, cheesy and delicious croquette cakes make a wonderful lunch or light supper when served with a fresh side salad and accompanied by hunks of crusty bread.

PREP: 10 MINS
COOK: 10 MINS
SERVES: 4

1 x 500g pack pre-cooked mashed potatoes
6 slices ham, chopped
1 cup (140g) pre-grated Cheddar cheese
1 tsp English mustard
4 spring onions, finely sliced
2 heaped tbsp plain flour
1 egg
1 cup (45g) panko breadcrumbs
vegetable oil, for frying
salad and crusty French bread, to serve (optional)

1 Crumble the mashed potato into a large bowl, then add the ham, cheese, mustard, spring onions and flour and mix well to bring everything together.
2 Turn the mixture out onto a clean work surface and divide it into 2 halves. Using your hands, divide each half into 4 equal portions, then form each portion into a ball. Once you have formed 8 balls, use your hands to press them down into thick patties.
3 Set 2 shallow bowls on the work surface. Crack the egg into the first bowl and beat lightly to combine. Put the panko breadcrumbs in the second bowl.
4 Working with 1 croquette cake at a time, dip the cakes first in the beaten egg, then in the breadcrumbs to coat completely. Set aside on a plate or a sheet of baking paper while you coat the remaining cakes.

IF YOU'RE MAKING AHEAD TO *Freeze*...**SKIP TO THE BOTTOM**

IF YOU'RE COOKING *Now*... Preheat the oven to 180°C/350°F/gas mark 4. Set a frying pan over a medium heat and add 1cm/½ inch of vegetable oil to the base to heat. Once the oil is at temperature (you can check by adding a few of the breadcrumbs and checking that they sizzle), cook the croquette cakes in batches for 2–3 minutes on each side, until golden. Set aside while you cook the remaining cakes. Once all the cakes are fried, transfer to a foil-lined baking sheet and place in the oven to cook for 6 minutes, until piping hot all the way through. Serve the cakes hot, with salad and a hunk of crusty French bread on the side, if you like.

IF YOU'RE MAKING AHEAD TO *Freeze*...
Once coated in breadcrumbs, place the croquette cakes on a foil-lined baking tray, then place the tray in the freezer for 1 hour to flash freeze. Once frozen, transfer the cakes to a large, labelled freezer bag and freeze flat for up to 3 months.

Then... These can be cooked straight from frozen. Set a frying pan over a medium heat and add 1cm/½ inch of vegetable oil to the base to heat. Once the oil is at temperature (you can check by adding a few of the breadcrumbs and checking that they sizzle), cook the croquette cakes in batches for 2–3 minutes on each side, until golden. Set aside while you cook the remaining cakes. Once all the cakes are fried, transfer to a foil-lined baking sheet and place in an oven preheated to 180°C/350°F/gas mark 4 to cook for 12 minutes, until piping hot all the way through.

SMOKY SWEET POTATO & SALMON CAKES

The chipotle paste in these salmon fishcakes imparts a mellow smoky warmth that contrasts well with the sweetness of the sweet potato mash. Cook straight from frozen and serve with salad for a quick and easy midweek dinner or light lunch.

PREP: 5 MINS
COOK: 30 MINS
SERVES: 4

640g (1½ packs) pre-cooked sweet potato mash
1 x 170g can pink salmon, drained and flaked, skin and big bones removed
1–2 tsp chipotle paste
2 eggs, beaten
1 cup (45g) panko breadcrumbs
oil, for drizzling
salt and freshly ground black pepper
salad, to serve (optional)

1 Crumble the mashed potato into a large bowl, then add the salmon, chipotle paste and a generous grinding of salt and pepper. Mix well to bring everything together.
2 Turn the mixture out onto a clean work surface and divide it into 2 halves. Using your hands, divide each half into 4 equal portions, then form each portion into a ball. Once you have formed 8 balls, use your hands to press them down into thick patties.
3 Set 2 shallow bowls on the work surface. Crack the eggs into the first bowl and beat lightly to combine. Put the panko breadcrumbs in the second bowl.
4 Working with 1 at a time, dip the fishcakes first in the beaten egg, then in the breadcrumbs to coat completely. Set aside on a plate or a sheet of baking paper while you coat the remaining fishcakes.

IF YOU'RE MAKING AHEAD TO *Freeze*...**SKIP TO THE BOTTOM**

IF YOU'RE COOKING *Now*... Lay the fishcakes on a foil-lined baking sheet and drizzle with a little oil. Transfer to an oven preheated to 180°C/350°F/gas mark 4 to bake for 30 minutes, until crisp and golden. Serve hot with salad on the side, if you like.

IF YOU'RE MAKING AHEAD TO *Freeze*... Lay the fishcakes on a foil-lined baking sheet and put the whole tray in the freezer to flash freeze for 1 hour, then transfer to a large, labelled freezer bag and freeze for up to 3 months.

Then... These can be cooked straight from frozen. Lay the frozen fishcakes on a foil-lined baking sheet, drizzle over a little oil and transfer to an oven preheated to 180°C/350°F/gas mark and bake for 40 minutes, until crisp, golden and piping hot all of the way through.

GARLICKY BREADED MUSHROOMS

These little breaded mushrooms are crunchy morsels of deliciousness! They are brilliant as a snack in front of the TV on a Friday night but are so good that I would also serve them as a canapé or starter at a dinner party. I serve them with a garlicky aioli alongside for dipping and dunking.

PREP: 10 MINS
COOK: 15 MINS
SERVES: 4

4 tbsp plain flour
2 eggs
2 cups (90g) panko breadcrumbs
1 tsp smoked paprika
1 tsp garlic powder
1 tsp dried oregano
1 tsp salt
300g button mushrooms
oil, for drizzling
freshly ground black pepper

For the aioli:
½ cup (120ml) mayonnaise
2 tsp frozen chopped garlic
1 tsp frozen chopped parsley

1 Line a large baking sheet with baking paper.
2 Set three shallow bowls on the work surface. Put the flour in the first bowl. Crack the eggs into the second bowl and beat lightly to combine. Put the panko breadcrumbs, paprika, garlic powder, oregano, salt and a grinding of pepper in the third bowl and stir to combine.
3 Working with one mushroom at a time, dip the mushrooms first in the flour, then in the beaten egg and finally in the breadcrumbs to thoroughly coat. Lay the mushrooms on the prepared baking sheet while you coat the remainder in the same way.

IF YOU'RE MAKING AHEAD TO *Freeze*...**SKIP TO THE BOTTOM**

IF YOU'RE COOKING *Now*... Drizzle the mushrooms with a little oil, then transfer the baking sheet to an oven preheated to 200°C/400°F/gas mark 6 and cook for 15 minutes, until golden. While the mushrooms are cooking, make the aioli by combining the mayonnaise, garlic and parsley in a bowl and mixing well to combine. Serve the mushrooms hot with the aioli alongside for dipping.

IF YOU'RE MAKING AHEAD TO *Freeze*...
Place the baking sheet with the mushrooms in the freezer to flash freeze for 1 hour, then transfer the mushrooms to a large, labelled freezer bag and freeze for up to 3 months.

Then... Lay the frozen mushrooms on a baking paper-lined baking sheet and drizzle with a little oil. Transfer to an oven preheated to 200°C/400°F/gas mark 6 and cook for 20–25 minutes, until golden and piping hot all the way through. Make the aioli and serve the mushrooms as described above.

TUNA-FILLED POTATO SKINS

I always have a stash of these in the freezer for lunches or after-school meals on busy days.
They are quick, tasty and kids will love them.

PREP: 10 MINS
COOK: 30–35 MINS
SERVES: 4

4 medium-sized baking potatoes
1 tbsp olive or vegetable oil
100g cream cheese
4 spring onions, finely sliced
1 x 200g can sweetcorn, drained
2 x 145g cans tuna, drained
1 cup (90g) pre-grated Cheddar
  cheese
salt and freshly ground black pepper

1 Preheat the oven to 180°C/350°F/gas mark 4 and line a baking sheet with foil.
2 Prick the potatoes all over with a fork and microwave on high for 12 minutes, or longer if necessary, until tender.
3 Slice the potatoes in half and, being careful not to burn your hands, scoop out the flesh into a bowl, leaving the potato skins intact.
4 Lay the hollowed-out potato skins on a baking sheet and drizzle with the olive or vegetable oil. Transfer to the oven and bake for 8 minutes, until crisp.
5 Meanwhile, put the cream cheese, spring onions, sweetcorn, tuna and a generous grinding of salt and pepper in a bowl and mix well to combine.
6 Divide the filling mixture between the potato skins.

IF YOU'RE MAKING AHEAD TO *Freeze*...**SKIP TO THE BOTTOM**

IF YOU'RE COOKING *Now*... Scatter the grated cheese over the filled potato skins and bake at 180°C/350°F/gas mark 4 for 15–20 minutes, until the cheese is melted and bubbling.

IF YOU'RE MAKING AHEAD TO *Freeze*...
Set the filled potato skins aside until completely cool on the baking sheet, then put the whole baking sheet in the freezer for 1 hour to flash freeze. After an hour, transfer the potato skins to a large, labelled freezer bag and freeze flat for up to 3 months.

Then... These can be cooked straight from frozen. Lay the frozen potato skins on a foil-lined baking sheet and transfer to an oven preheated to 180°C/350°F/gas mark 4 for 30 minutes. Remove the tray from the oven, scatter over the cheese and return to the oven for another 10 minutes, until the cheese is melted and the skins are piping hot all the way through.

ARRABIATA PASTA SAUCE

This wonderfully versatile sauce can be used over pasta, in meatball subs or anything you fancy. It is great to have a batch ready in the freezer for easy lunches or dinners as it is really economical, so is perfect for the when you're waiting for payday at the end of the month.

PREP: 5 MINS
COOK: 20 MINS
SERVES: 4

1 tbsp olive or vegetable oil
2 tsp frozen chopped garlic
½ tsp dried chilli flakes
1 x 400g tin chopped tomatoes
1 x 500g carton passata
½ cup (120ml) vegetable stock
1 tsp sugar
salt and freshly ground black pepper
cooked pasta, to serve (optional)

1   Heat the oil in a large pan over a medium heat, add the garlic and cook, stirring, for 1 minute, then add the chilli flakes, chopped tomatoes, passata, vegetable stock, sugar and a generous grinding of salt and pepper. Bring the mixture to the boil, then reduce the heat to a gentle simmer and leave to cook, stirring occasionally, for 20 minutes.

IF YOU'RE MAKING AHEAD TO *Freeze*...**SKIP TO THE BOTTOM**

IF YOU'RE SERVING *Now*... Simply use the sauce to dress cooked pasta, top pizzas or spoon into meatball subs.

IF YOU'RE MAKING AHEAD TO *Freeze*...
Set the sauce aside to cool to room temperature, then spoon into a large, labelled freezer bag and freeze flat for up to 3 months.

Then... This can be defrosted first or reheated straight from frozen. If defrosting first, simply remove the sauce from the freezer the day before you want to serve it and leave to defrost overnight in the fridge, then transfer to a pan over a medium heat until piping hot. If reheating from frozen, tip the frozen sauce into a saucepan over a low heat. Heat gently, breaking the sauce up with a wooden spoon as you do, until melted and piping hot all the way through.

10 Chicken MEALS IN 1 HOUR

↓

YOU WILL BE MAKING

| BUTTER CHICKEN | BFC CORNFLAKE CHICKEN | PESTO & MOZZARELLA STUFFED CHICKEN BREASTS | SMOKY CHICKEN BURGERS | CHICKEN MEATBALLS |

Since my first book came out, so many of my followers have been asking me for another chicken 10 meals in 1 hour, so here it is! These are perfect family meals to fill your freezer with and the menu includes guaranteed crowd pleasers to keep the whole family happy. These recipes can be found elsewhere in the book as single recipes but in this section, they are woven together and scaled up into double portions to help you fill your freezer in one dedicated batching session. Read through the recipe first to get a general view of how it is going to work and what equipment you will need to have on hand. The shopping list below includes everything you will need, and I've scaled up the ingredients so you know what pack sizes to buy of each. Lay the ingredients out in piles according to the groupings under the ingredients heading overleaf, then follow the numbered guide and you can't go wrong!

Shopping list

Fresh

1 x 250g block butter

24 skinless, boneless chicken breasts

1¼ cups (300ml) double cream

2kg minced chicken or turkey (7% fat)

2 x 240g balls mozzarella cheese

8 rashers smoked bacon

Frozen

1 x 500g pack frozen chopped onions

1 x 100g pack frozen chopped garlic

1 x 100g pack frozen chopped ginger

1 x 100g pack frozen chopped chilli

Storecupboard

1 jar garam masala

1 jar ground cumin

1 tube tomato purée

2 x 400g cans chopped tomatoes

1 pack chicken stock cubes

1 pack cornflakes

1 small jar garlic granules

1 small jar smoked paprika

12 eggs

1 pack dried breadcrumbs

1 jar dried oregano

1 jar pesto

INGREDIENTS

GET ORGANISED! Before you start make sure that your kitchen surfaces are cleared down, then lay all the ingredients out in individual piles according to the groupings on this page. It is also a good idea to prepare and label your freezer bags.

BUTTER CHICKEN

2 tbsp butter
2 cups (230g) frozen chopped onions
4 tsp frozen chopped garlic
4 tsp frozen chopped ginger
4 tsp frozen chopped chilli
8 skinless, boneless chicken breasts, cut into bite-sized pieces
4 tsp garam masala
4 tsp ground cumin
4 tbsp tomato purée
2 x 400g cans chopped tomatoes
1 cup (240ml) chicken stock
1 cup (240ml) double cream

BFC CORNFLAKE CHICKEN

6 cups (210g) cornflakes
2 tsp garlic granules
2 tsp smoked paprika
1 tsp salt
4 eggs, beaten
8 skinless, boneless chicken breasts, each breast cut into 3–4 long strips

PESTO & MOZZARELLA STUFFED CHICKEN BREASTS

8 skinless, boneless chicken breasts
8 tsp pesto
2 balls mozzarella cheese, cut into 4 halves
8 rashers bacon

SMOKY CHICKEN BURGERS

800g minced chicken or turkey
2 tsp garlic granules
2 tsp smoked paprika
¾ cup (35g) dried breadcrumbs
1 tsp salt (optional)
2 eggs

CHICKEN MEATBALLS

800g minced chicken or turkey
2 tsp garlic granules
4 tsp dried oregano
1 tsp salt (optional)
¾ cup (35g) breadcrumbs
2 eggs

METHOD

BUTTER CHICKEN

1 Melt the butter in a large saucepan over a medium heat. Once melted, add the onion, garlic, ginger, chilli and chopped chicken breasts and cook, stirring continuously, for 4–5 minutes, until the onions are soft and translucent and the chicken is sealed.

2 Add the garam masala, ground cumin, tomato purée, chopped tomatoes, chicken stock and double cream to the pan and stir to combine. Bring the mixture to the boil, then reduce the heat to a simmer and leave to cook for 25 minutes, stirring occasionally.

BFC CORNFLAKE CHICKEN

3 Put the cornflakes in a large freezer bag and bash with a rolling pin to make fine crumbs. Transfer the cornflake crumbs to a shallow bowl along with the garlic granules, smoked paprika and salt, and stir to combine. Set another bowl next to the first and add the beaten eggs.

4 Working with one piece at a time, dip the chicken first in the egg then in the breadcrumbs, ensuring that it is well coated in both. Divide the coated chicken between 2 foil-lined baking sheets and repeat with the remaining pieces.

5 Transfer the baking sheets to the freezer for 1 hour to allow the chicken pieces to firm up. Once part frozen, transfer the chicken to a large, labelled freezer bag and freeze flat for up to 3 months.

BUTTER CHICKEN CONTINUED...

6 Give the chicken a stir and add a splash of water if the mixture looks a little dry. Clean down the kitchen surfaces, putting away anything used for making the BFC Cornflake Chicken.

PESTO & MOZZARELLA STUFFED CHICKEN BREASTS

7 Working with 1 chicken breast at a time, use a sharp knife to carefully slice a pocket into the thick end of each breast, being careful that your knife does not slice through the breast and puncture the other side. Repeat with the remaining 7 chicken breasts.

8 Cut each of the 4 mozzarella ball halves into 4 even slices. Fill the pocket of each chicken breast with 1 teaspoon of pesto and 2 slices of mozzarella, then wrap a slice of bacon around each of the stuffed chicken breasts.

9 Cut 8 squares of foil, roughly 30 x 30cm (12 x 12 inches) and place an uncooked, stuffed chicken breast in the centre of each. Bring up the edges of the foil and crimp together to seal the chicken inside. Divide the foil-wrapped chicken breasts between 2 large, labelled freezer bags and freeze flat for up to 3 months.

10   The butter chicken should now be cooked. Remove from the heat and set aside to cool to room temperature. Wipe down the kitchen surfaces and clear away anything used to prepare the Butter Chicken or the Pesto and Mozzarella Stuffed Chicken Breasts.

SMOKY CHICKEN BURGERS

11   Put all the ingredients in a large mixing bowl and use your hands to bring together until well combined. Turn out onto a clean work surface, then divide the mixture into 8 even pieces. Using your hands, roll each piece into a ball, then press down to form a burger shape roughly the same circumference as a burger bun.

12   Cut 8 squares of baking paper roughly the same size of the burgers, then pile the burgers up in stacks of 4, placing a square of parchment between each one. Divide the burgers between 2 labelled freezer bags and freeze for up to 3 months.

CHICKEN MEATBALLS

13   Combine all the ingredients in a large mixing bowl and use your hands to mix together well, ensuring that the herbs and breadcrumbs are evenly distributed throughout the chicken. Turn the mixture out onto a clean work surface and divide into 2 equal portions. Divide each half into 8, then each piece of meat in half again so that you have 32 equal pieces. Roll into balls with your hands.

14   Divide the uncooked meatballs between 2 large, labelled freezer bags and freeze flat for up to 3 months.

BUTTER CHICKEN CONTINUED...

15   Once the butter chicken has cooled to room temperature, ladle into 2 large, labelled freezer bags and freeze flat for up to 3 months.

Congratulations
You now have 10 evening meals ready for the freezer!

WHEN YOU COME TO COOK

BUTTER CHICKEN

Remove the butter chicken from the freezer and leave to defrost fully in the fridge, ideally overnight. Once defrosted, tip the butter chicken into a large pan and reheat over a medium heat for 10–15 minutes, stirring occasionally, until piping hot all of the way through.

BFC CORNFLAKE CHICKEN

The chicken can be cooked directly from frozen. Preheat the oven to 180°C/350°F/gas mark 4 and line a baking sheet with baking paper. Transfer the frozen chicken pieces to the prepared baking sheet in a single layer, drizzle over a little oil then cook in the oven for 20–25 minutes, until crisp, golden and piping hot all of the way through.

PESTO & MOZZARELLA STUFFED CHICKEN BREASTS

Remove the chicken breasts from the freezer and leave to defrost in the fridge, ideally overnight. Once defrosted, preheat the oven to 180°C/350°F/gas mark 4 and unwrap the tops of the foil parcels to expose the chicken breasts. Lay on a baking sheet and transfer to the oven to cook for 30–35 minutes, until piping hot all the way through.

SMOKY CHICKEN BURGERS

Remove as many burgers as you need from the freezer and leave to defrost in the fridge overnight. Once defrosted, preheat the oven to 180°C/350°F/gas mark 4 and line a baking sheet with foil. Remove the paper backing from the burgers and lay on the baking tray, then cook for 20–25 minutes, until golden and cooked through.

CHICKEN MEATBALLS

Remove the meatballs from the freezer and leave to defrost fully in the fridge, ideally overnight. Once defrosted, preheat the oven to 180°C/350°F/gas mark 4 and line a baking tray with foil. Lay the meatballs of the baking sheet and drizzle with a little oil, then transfer to the oven to cook for 20–25 minutes, until golden and cooked through.

WEEKNIGHT

CHICKEN & VEGETABLE FRICASSEE

PREP: 10 MINS
COOK: 35 MINS
SERVES 4

2 tbsp olive or vegetable oil

4–6 skinless, boneless chicken thighs

1 cup (115g) frozen chopped onions

2 carrots, peeled and finely chopped

2 cups (140g) chestnut mushrooms, sliced

2 tsp frozen chopped garlic

2 tbsp plain flour

1½ cups (360ml) chicken stock

2 tsp wholegrain mustard

1 cup (140g) frozen sweetcorn

1 tbsp runny honey

1 heaped tbsp crème fraîche

salt and freshly ground black pepper

mashed potatoes, to serve (optional)

1   Heat 1 tablespoon of the oil in a large, deep-sided frying pan over a medium heat, then add the chicken thighs and cook for 3–4 minutes on each side, until golden. Transfer the chicken thighs to a plate and return the pan to the heat.

2   Add the remaining tablespoon of oil to the pan, then add the onions, carrots, mushrooms and garlic and cook for 2–3 minutes, until the vegetables have softened.

3   Add the flour to the pan and stir to combine with the vegetables, cook for a minute or so, stirring, to cook out the flour. Pour the chicken stock into the pan, reduce the heat to low and cook for 5 minutes, stirring with a whisk as you do, until you have a smooth, thickened sauce.

4   Add the mustard and sweetcorn to the pan and stir to combine, then return the chicken thighs to the sauce and leave to bubble away for 35 minutes.

5   Remove the pan from the heat and stir through the honey, crème fraîche and a generous grinding of salt and pepper.

IF YOU'RE MAKING AHEAD TO *Freeze*...**SKIP TO THE BOTTOM**

IF YOU'RE SERVING *Now*... Spoon the fricassee into serving bowls and serve hot with mashed potatoes alongside, if you like.

Half & Half

Reduce the chicken by half and add an extra cup (70g) of mushrooms and an extra cup (140g) of sweetcorn to the mixture.

IF YOU'RE MAKING AHEAD TO *Freeze*...
Set the pan aside until the fricassee has cooled to room temperature, then ladle into a large, labelled freezer bag and freeze flat for up to 3 months.

Then... This can be cooked from frozen or defrosted first. If defrosting, remove the fricassee from the freezer and leave to defrost in the fridge, ideally overnight. Once defrosted, tip into a large saucepan over a medium heat and reheat for 5–10 minutes, until piping hot all the way through. If cooking from frozen, simply tip the frozen fricassee into a large saucepan over a low heat with a splash of water and cook, breaking up the fricassee with a wooden spoon as it thaws, until completely defrosted and piping hot all of the way through. Serve hot, with mashed potatoes alongside.

GARLIC BUTTER KYIV

Chicken Kyiv is an absolute family favourite, and it's little wonder why – succulent breaded chicken filled with an oozing sauce of garlicky buttery goodness. These are so much tastier than the shop-bought variety and people will be really impressed when you tell them you've made your own!

PREP: 15 MINS
COOK: 18–20 MINS
SERVES 4

4 heaped tbsp soft butter
2 tsp frozen chopped garlic
2 tsp frozen parsley
4 heaped tbsp plain flour
2 eggs
1 cup (45g) breadcrumbs
4 skinless, boneless chicken breasts
1 tbsp olive or vegetable oil
salt and freshly ground black pepper
potato wedges and side salad, to
   serve (optional)

1 To make the garlic butter, combine the butter, garlic and parsley in a small bowl and beat together until well combined. Tip the butter onto the centre of a sheet of clingfilm, then use the clingfilm to roll the butter into a sausage shape. Twist the ends of the clingfilm to seal, then transfer the butter to the fridge to firm up for at least 10 minutes.

2 Set three shallow bowl next to each other on the counter. Add the flour to the first bowl along with a generous grinding of salt and pepper, beat the eggs into the second bowl and add the breadcrumbs to the third.

3 Working with 1 chicken breast at a time, use a sharp knife to carefully slice a pocket into the thick end of each breast, being careful that your knife does not slice through the breast and puncture the other side. Repeat with the remaining 3 chicken breasts.

4 Slice the cooled butter into 4 equal pieces, then push 1 of the pieces of butter into the pocket in each chicken breast. Once stuffed with the butter, dip the chicken breasts first in the flour, then in the eggs, then in the breadcrumbs, ensuring that each chicken breast is well coated at each stage.

IF YOU'RE MAKING AHEAD TO *Freeze*...**SKIP TO THE BOTTOM**

IF YOU'RE COOKING *Now*... Preheat the oven to 200°C/400°F/gas mark 6 and line a baking sheet with foil. Heat the oil in a frying pan over a medium heat, then add the Kyivs and cook for 2–3 minutes on each side, until the breadcrumbs are golden. Handle the chicken carefully so as not to squeeze out the butter. Once golden, transfer the chicken breasts to the prepared baking sheet and bake in the oven for 15–20 minutes, until tender and cooked through. Serve the Kyivs with potato wedges and a side salad alongside, if you like.

IF YOU'RE MAKING AHEAD TO *Freeze*...
Place the uncooked Kyivs in a large, labelled freezer bag and freeze flat for up to 3 months.

Then... Remove the Kyivs from the freezer and leave to defrost in the fridge, ideally overnight. Once defrosted, preheat the oven to 200°C/400°F/gas mark 6, then fry, bake and serve the Kyivs as described above.

HALF & HALF LENTIL BOLOGNESE

Lentils are such a great budget ingredient – they are healthy, absorb flavour brilliantly and are ideal for bulking out a mince-based dish so that a little bit of meat goes a long way. They also keep for ages, so I like to buy mine in the international food aisle in the supermarkets, where they are sold in big bags for a cheaper price.

PREP: 5 MINS
COOK: 30 MINS
SERVES 4

1 tbsp olive oil
2 cups (115g) frozen chopped onions
1 tsp frozen chopped garlic
250g lean minced beef
1 cup (70g) grated carrot
2 cups (140g) frozen sliced mushrooms
1 cup (200g) dried red lentils
1 x 500g carton passata
1 x 400g tin chopped tomatoes
1 tbsp tomato purée
2 tsp dried oregano
salt and freshly ground black pepper
cooked spaghetti, to serve (optional)

1 Heat the oil in a large pan over a medium heat, then add the onions and garlic and cook, stirring continuously, for 2–3 minutes, until softened.
2 Add the minced beef, carrots and mushrooms to the pan and cook, breaking up the mince with a wooden spoon or spatula as you do, until the minced is browned.
3 Add the lentils, passata, chopped tomatoes, tomato purée and dried oregano to the pan and stir to combine. Bring the mixture to the boil, then reduce to a simmer and leave to cook for 30 minutes, stirring occasionally, until the lentils are tender and the Bolognese is nice and thick. Season with salt and pepper, then remove the pan from the heat.

IF YOU'RE MAKING AHEAD TO *Freeze*...**SKIP TO THE BOTTOM**

IF YOU'RE SERVING *Now*... Ladle the Bolognese into pasta bowls over a serving of cooked spaghetti. Serve hot.

Zhuzh it up...
Stir some fresh basil through the sauce before serving and top with freshly grated Parmesan cheese.

IF YOU'RE MAKING AHEAD TO *Freeze*...
Set the pan aside until the Bolognese has cooled to room temperature, then ladle into a large, labelled freezer bag and freeze flat for up to 3 months.

Then... This can be cooked from frozen or defrosted first. If defrosting, remove the bag from the freezer and leave to defrost in the fridge, ideally overnight. Once defrosted, transfer the Bolognese to a large saucepan and reheat over a medium heat, stirring occasionally, for 5–10 minutes, until piping hot. If cooking from frozen, simply tip the frozen Bolognese into a large saucepan over a low heat with a splash of water and cook, breaking up the Bolognese with a wooden spoon as it thaws, until completely defrosted and piping hot all of the way through. Serve with cooked spaghetti alongside.

CHEESY HIDDEN VEG PASTA BAKE

This is a great midweek family well that works brilliantly if your children are vegetable averse. Coated in a rich and creamy cheese sauce, these veggies feel like a real treat and are sure to convert even the most determined vegetable dodger!

PREP: 15 MINS
COOK: 35 MINS
SERVES 4

350g dried penne pasta
½ head broccoli, cut into small florets
50g butter
scant ½ cup (50g) plain flour
2½ cups (600ml) milk
2 cups (280g) pre-grated Cheddar cheese
1 tsp English mustard
1 x 200g tin sweetcorn, drained
½ cup (23g) breadcrumbs
salt and freshly ground black pepper
garlic bread and green salad, to serve (optional)

1 Put the pasta in a large pan over a medium heat and pour over boiling water to cover. Bring to the boil, then reduce the heat to a simmer and leave to cook for 6 minutes. Add the broccoli florets to the pan and cook for an additional 2 minutes, until the pasta and broccoli are almost tender but still retaining some bite. Drain through a colander and tip into a large baking dish in an even layer, ensuring that the broccoli is evenly distributed throughout the pasta. Set aside.

2 To make the sauce, melt the butter in a large pan over a low heat. Add the flour to the pan and stir with the butter to form a thick paste. Keep stirring for around a minute to cook out the flour, then gradually add the milk, thickening and whisking between each addition until you have a thick, glossy sauce.

3 Remove the pan from the heat, then add 1½ cups (210g) of the grated cheese along with the mustard, sweetcorn and a generous grinding of salt and pepper. Pour the sauce over the top of the pasta and broccoli and give everything a gentle stir in the dish to ensure the sauce is coating the pasta and broccoli. Scatter the remaining ½ cup (70g) of cheese and the breadcrumbs over the top

IF YOU'RE MAKING AHEAD TO *Freeze*...**SKIP TO THE BOTTOM**

IF YOU'RE COOKING *Now*... Preheat the oven to 180°C/350°F/gas mark 4, then transfer the pasta bake to the hot oven to cook for 35 minutes, until golden and bubbling. Spoon into serving bowls and serve hot, with garlic bread and salad leaves alongside, if you like.

IF YOU'RE MAKING AHEAD TO *Freeze*...
Set the unbaked pasta bake aside until cooled to room temperature, then cover with a lid or wrap in a layer of clingfilm followed by a layer of foil, label and freeze flat for up to 3 months.

Then... This can be cooked from frozen. Preheat the oven to 180°C/350°F/gas mark 4, cover the baking dish with foil (removing any clingfilm if you used it to wrap the pasta bake before freezing) and transfer to the oven for 30 minutes, then remove the foil and cook for another 30 minutes, until golden and bubbling.

MEXICAN BEEF PASTA BAKE

Adding the vibrant flavours of Mexico to a pasta bake is a great way to add a hint of spice that the whole family will love.

PREP: 15 MINS
COOK: 25–30 MINS
SERVES 4

1 tbsp vegetable or olive oil
1 cup (115g) frozen chopped onion
2 tsp frozen chopped garlic
150g minced beef
1 x 30g pack taco seasoning
1 x 500g carton passata
2 x 400g tin chopped tomatoes
1 cup (70g) frozen sliced peppers
300g dried pasta
1½ cups (210g) pre-grated
  mozzarella cheese

MAKE IT
Veggie!
Substitute the beef mince
with a plant-based
alternative for an easy
veggie supper!

1 Heat the oil in a large pan over a medium heat, then add the onions and garlic and cook for 2–3 minutes, until soft. Add the beef mince to the pan and cook, breaking up with a wooden spoon as you do, until browned.

2 Add the taco seasoning, passata, chopped tomatoes and peppers to the pan and stir to combine. Bring the mixture to the boil, then reduce the heat to a simmer and leave to cook for 15 minutes, stirring occasionally.

3 While the mince is cooking, put the pasta in a large pan over a medium heat and pour over boiling water to cover. Bring to the boil, then reduce the heat to a simmer and leave to cook for 8 minutes, until almost tender but still retaining some bite. Drain and set aside.

4 Once the mince mixture has finished cooking, remove from the heat and stir through the pasta. Once combined, tip the mixture into a large baking dish and scatter over the grated mozzarella.

IF YOU'RE MAKING AHEAD TO *Freeze*...**SKIP TO THE BOTTOM**

IF YOU'RE COOKING *Now*... Preheat the oven to 180°C/350°F/gas mark 4, then transfer the pasta bake to the hot oven to cook for 25–30 minutes, until golden and bubbling. Spoon into serving bowls and serve hot, with garlic bread and salad leaves alongside, if you like.

IF YOU'RE MAKING AHEAD TO *Freeze*...
Set the unbaked pasta bake aside until cooled to room temperature, then cover with a lid or wrap in a layer of clingfilm followed by a layer of foil, label and freeze flat for up to 3 months.

Then... This can be cooked from frozen. Preheat the oven to 180°C/350°F/gas mark 4, cover the baking dish with foil (removing any clingfilm if you used it to wrap the pasta bake before freezing) and transfer to the oven for 40 minutes, then remove the foil and cook for another 20 minutes, until golden and bubbling.

10
Minced-based
MEALS IN
1 HOUR

↓

YOU WILL BE MAKING

| MEXICAN BEEF NACHO TOPPER | MINCED BEEF HOTPOT | BEEF KEEMA | CHEESEBURGER SAUSAGE ROLL | SPICED BEEF SKEWERS |

Minced beef is far cheaper than other kinds of red meat, making it great for family cooking. These recipes can be found elsewhere in the book but in this section they are woven together and scaled up into double portions to help you fill your freezer in one dedicated batching session. Read through the recipe first to get a general view of how it is going to work and what equipment you will need to have on hand. The shopping list below includes everything you will need, and I've scaled up the ingredients so you know what pack sizes to buy of each. Lay the ingredients out in piles according to the groupings under the ingredients heading overleaf, then follow the numbered guide and you can't go wrong!

Shopping list

Fresh

4.5kg minced beef (20% fat)

1 x 450g pack pre-grated Cheddar cheese

2 sheets pre-rolled puff pastry

Frozen

2 x 500g packs frozen chopped onions

1 x 100g pack frozen chopped garlic

1 x 500g pack frozen chopped carrots

1 x 1kg pack frozen peas

1 x 500g pack frozen sliced peppers

1 x 100g pack frozen diced ginger

Storecupboard

1 small bottle olive or vegetable oil

2 tubes tomato purée

1 jar dried rosemary

1 jar dried bay leaves

1 small pack plain flour

1 pack beef stock cubes

1 bottle Worcestershire sauce

2 x 30g packs taco seasoning

2 x 395g tins beans in chilli sauce

1 jar medium curry powder

4 x 400g tins chopped tomatoes

1 bottle American mustard

6 eggs

1 bottle ketchup

1 jar garlic granules

1 jar onion powder

1 jar paprika

1 jar ground cumin

16 x 18cm (7 inch) wooden or metal skewers

INGREDIENTS PER RECIPE

GET ORGANISED! Before you start make sure that your kitchen surfaces are cleared down, then lay all the ingredients out in individual piles according to the groupings on this page. It is also a good idea to prepare and label your freezer bags.

MEXICAN BEEF NACHO TOPPER

2 tbsp oil
2 cups (230g) frozen chopped onions
3 tsp frozen chopped garlic
500g minced beef
2 x 30g packets taco seasoning
2 x 395g tins mixed beans in chilli sauce
4 tbsp tomato purée
2 cups (350g) frozen sliced peppers

To serve

2 cups (180g) pre-grated Cheddar cheese
2 x 200g packs tortilla chips

MINCED BEEF HOTPOT

2 cups (230g) frozen chopped onions
3 tsp frozen chopped garlic
1kg minced beef
2 cups (380g) frozen chopped carrots
2 cups (310g) frozen peas
4 tbsp tomato purée
2 tbsp dried rosemary
2 bay leaves
4 tbsp plain flour
6 cups (1.4 litres) beef stock
2 tbsp Worcestershire sauce
salt and freshly ground black pepper

To serve

4–6 medium sized potatoes, thinly sliced

BEEF KEEMA

2 tbsp oil
2 cups (230g) frozen chopped onions
4 tsp frozen chopped garlic
4 tsp frozen chopped ginger
1kg minced beef
4 tbsp medium curry powder
4 x 400g tins chopped tomatoes
1 cup (240ml) beef stock (use 2 cubes)
2 cups (310g) frozen peas

CHEESEBURGER ROLL

1kg beef mince
4 tbsp Worcestershire sauce
2 tsp American mustard
3 eggs
2 sheets pre-rolled puff pastry
2 cups (180g) pre-grated Cheddar cheese
4 tbsp ketchup

SPICED BEEF SKEWERS

1kg minced beef
2 tsp garlic powder
2 tsp onion powder
2 tsp paprika
2 tsp ground cumin
2 tbsp tomato purée
1 tsp salt
1 egg

METHOD

MEXICAN BEEF NACHO TOPPER & MINCED BEEF HOTPOT

1   Heat 2 tablespoons of oil in a very large pan over a medium heat , then add the onions, garlic and beef from both recipes and stir to combine. Cook the beef, stirring occasionally, for 5 minutes, until browned.

BEEF KEEMA

2   While the beef for the first 2 recipes is browning, heat the oil for the Beef Keema in a separate pan, then add the onions, garlic, ginger and minced beef and cook for 5 minutes, until the beef has browned.

MEXICAN BEEF NACHO TOPPER CONTINUED...

3   Drain off any fat from the cooked minced beef, then scoop 2½ cups of the mixture into a separate bowl – this will be the Mexican Beef Nacho Topper.

MINCED BEEF HOTPOT CONTINUED...

4   Add the carrots, peas, tomato purée, dried rosemary, bay leaves and flour to the remaining beef mixture in the saucepan and mix well. Add the beef stock and Worcestershire sauce, season well and leave to simmer for around 20 minutes.

BEEF KEEMA CONTINUED...

5   Drain off any fat from the cooked minced beef, then add the curry powder, chopped tomatoes, beef stock and peas to the pan. Stir to combine, bring the mixture to the boil, then reduce to a simmer and leave to cook, stirring occasionally, for 20 minutes.

MEXICAN BEEF NACHO TOPPER CONTINUED...

6   Add the taco seasoning, beans in chilli sauce, sliced frozen peppers and tomato purée to the cooked minced beef in the bowl and mix well. Divide the mixture between two labelled freezer bags and, once completely cool, seal and freeze flat for up to 3 months.

CHEESEBURGER SAUSAGE ROLL

7   Crack two of the eggs into a large mixing bowl and beat gently to combine, then add the minced beef, Worcestershire sauce, mustard and a generous grinding each of salt and pepper. Using your hands, combine the mixture until all the elements are well incorporated.

8   Unroll the sheets of puff pastry, keeping them on their baking paper linings, and set them on the work surface in front of you so that the wider edges are at the top and bottom. Using a sharp knife, lightly score a horizontal line through the middle of each sheet of pastry to divide it into 2 equal halves, being sure not to cut all the way through the pastry.

9   Leaving a 2.5cm (1in) border around the edge of the pastry, spoon half of the beef mixture into the centre of the top half of each pastry sheet (above the line you have just marked) and form it into an

even sausage shape with your hands, then sprinkle half the grated Cheddar over the top of each beef sausage in an even layer.

10   Leaving a 2.5cm (1in) border around the edge, evenly spread the tomato ketchup over the bottom half of the pastry sheet.

11   Crack the remaining egg into a small bowl and beat lightly to combine, then brush the border of pastry you have left around each sheet of pastry with the egg wash.

12   Bring the bottom half of each sheet of pastry up and over the top half to encase the beef sausage in the pastry, then use a fork to press all around the edges of the pastry to seal.

13   Wrap the uncooked sausage rolls up tightly in their baking paper wrappers, then wrap again in a couple of layers of clingfilm. Label clearly and freeze for up to 3 months.

MINCED BEEF HOTPOT & BEEF KEEMA CONTINUED...

14   Remove both pans from the heat and set aside until cooled to room temperature. Divide the beef hotpot between 2 large, labelled freezer bags and the keema between another 2 bags, then freeze all of the bags flat for up to 3 months.

SPICED BEEF SKEWERS

15   Put all the ingredients in a large bowl, then use your hands to bring everything together and ensure that all of the components are well distributed.

16   Divide the mixture into 16 equal pieces, then thread each piece onto a metal or wooden skewer (roughly 18cm/7 inches long). Use your fingers to squeeze each portion of meat along its skewer into a sausage shape.

17   Transfer the kofta skewers to a large, labelled freezer bag and freeze flat for up to 3 months.

Congratulations
You now have 10 evening meals ready for the freezer!

WHEN YOU COME TO COOK

MINCED BEEF HOTPOT

Remove the beef from the freezer and leave to fully defrost in the fridge, ideally overnight. Once defrosted, preheat the oven to 180°C/350°F/gas mark 4. Pour the beef mixture into a medium baking dish, then arrange the sliced potatoes over the surface, overlapping them slightly to create an even layer that covers right to the edges of the dish. Drizzle with a little oil, then transfer to the oven to bake for 30 minutes, until the potatoes are golden and the mince is bubbling. Spoon into bowls and serve hot.

MEXICAN BEEF NACHO TOPPER

Remove the bag from the freezer and leave to defrost in the fridge, ideally overnight. Once defrosted, tip the beef chilli into a large saucepan over a medium heat and reheat, stirring occasionally, for 5–10 minutes, until piping hot. While the chilli is reheating, put the tortilla chips in a large baking dish and warm in an oven preheated to 180°C/350°F/gas mark 4 for 5 minutes. Ladle the beef chilli over the top of the dish, scatter over the grated cheese then put the dish in the middle of the table for everyone to enjoy.

BEEF KEEMA

This can be cooked from frozen or defrosted first. If defrosting, remove the bag from the freezer and leave to defrost in the fridge, ideally overnight. Once defrosted, transfer the keema to a large saucepan and reheat over a medium heat, stirring occasionally, for 5–10 minutes, until piping hot. If cooking from frozen, simply tip the frozen keema into a large saucepan over a low heat with a splash of water and cook, breaking up the keema with a wooden spoon as it thaws, until completely defrosted and piping hot all of the way through. Serve with cooked basmati rice alongside.

CHEESEBURGER SAUSAGE ROLL

This can be cooked from frozen or defrosted first. To cook from frozen, simply unwrap the sausage roll, place on a baking paper-lined baking sheet and brush the top and sides with a little egg wash. Transfer to an oven preheated to 180°C/350°F/gas mark 4 and leave to bake for 1 hour, until golden, covering the sausage roll with foil if it starts to catch. To cook from defrosted, put the sausage roll in the fridge overnight and allow to defrost, then cook in the same way, but reduce the cooking time to 40 minutes.

SPICED BEEF SKEWERS

These can be cooked directly from frozen. Preheat the oven to 180°C/350°F/gas mark 4 and line a baking sheet with foil. Lay the kebabs on the baking sheet and transfer to the oven to bake for 25–30 minutes, until cooked through. Once cooked, slide the kebabs off the skewers and serve with flatbreads, hummus, feta and shredded lettuce.

VEGGIE SAUSAGE & CHICKPEA STEW

This warming, one-pot dish is fragrant with the flavour of fennel and paprika. Chickpeas are a great ingredient for bulking out any kind of soup or stew, as they are cheap, tasty and add immediate heft to a meal.

PREP: 10 MINS
COOK: 35 MINS
SERVES 4

1 tbsp vegetable or olive oil
8 vegetarian sausages
2 cups (230g) frozen chopped red
  onion
2 sticks celery, finely diced
2 tsp frozen chopped garlic
1 tsp dried fennel
1 x 400g can chickpeas, drained
2 x 400g tins chopped tomatoes
2 tsp smoked paprika
mashed potatoes, to serve
  (optional)

1 Heat the oil in a large, deep-sided frying pan over a medium heat. Once hot, add the sausages and cook, stirring, until browned on all sides. Transfer the sausages to a plate but keep the pan on the heat.

2 Add the onions and celery to the pan and cook for 6–8 minutes, until soft and translucent, then add the garlic, fennel, chickpeas, chopped tomatoes and paprika to the pan. Add a splash of water to each of the tomato tins and swirl around to loosen the juices, then tip this in also and stir to combine. Bring the mixture to the boil, then reduce to a simmer and leave to cook for 25 minutes, stirring occasionally. Return the sausages to the pan and stir to combine, then leave the stew to cook for a final 10 minutes.

IF YOU'RE MAKING AHEAD TO *Freeze*...**SKIP TO THE BOTTOM**

IF YOU'RE SERVING *Now*... Divide the stew between serving bowls and serve hot, either as it is or with mashed potatoes alongside.

Zhuzh it up...
Add a pinch of chilli flakes along with the fennel and paprika to add a punch of heat to the stew, and serve garnished with fresh chopped parsley.

IF YOU'RE MAKING AHEAD TO *Freeze*...
Set the stew aside to cool to room temperature, then transfer to a large labelled freezer bag and freeze flat for up to 3 months.

Then... Remove the stew from the freezer and leave to defrost fully in the fridge, ideally overnight. Once defrosted, tip the stew into a large pan and reheat over a medium hot for 5–10 minutes, until piping hot all the way through.

TUNA & SWEETCORN CARBONARA

This isn't a traditional carbonara, but the creamy blanket of sauce is perfect for spiking with lots of good stuff that your kids might otherwise turn their noses up at. I've suggested serving this with spaghetti, but use whatever pasta shape you have to hand.

PREP: 5 MINS
COOK: 8 MINS
SERVES 4

1 tbsp olive or vegetable oil
1 cup (115g) frozen chopped onions
2 tsp frozen chopped garlic
1¼ cups (300ml) double cream
2 x 145g tins tuna, drained and flaked
1 x 200g tin sweetcorn, drained
½ cup (40g) grated Parmesan cheese
salt and freshly ground black pepper
cooked spaghetti (or other pasta of your choice), to serve

1 Heat the oil in a large, deep-sided frying pan, then add the onions and garlic and cook for 2–3 minutes, until soft.
2 Add the double cream, tuna, sweetcorn, Parmesan and a generous grinding of salt and pepper, then stir to combine and cook for 2–3 minutes, until bubbling and slightly thickened.

IF YOU'RE MAKING AHEAD TO *Freeze*...**SKIP TO THE BOTTOM**

IF YOU'RE SERVING *Now*... Divide the cooked spaghetti between serving bowls then ladle over the sauce. Serve hot.

IF YOU'RE MAKING AHEAD TO *Freeze*...
Set the carbonara sauce aside to cool to room temperature, then transfer to a large, labelled freezer bag and freeze flat for up to 3 months.

Then... Remove the sauce from the freezer and leave to defrost in the fridge, ideally overnight. Once defrosted, tip the sauce into a pan and reheat slowly over a low heat to ensure the sauce doesn't split, until piping hot all the way through. Pour the sauce over cooked pasta and serve hot.

SWEET POTATO & CHICKPEA ONE POT

Recipes like this are what batching dreams are made of – simply combine all of the uncooked ingredients together in a freezer bag and you've got a family meal in the freezer ready to be cooked and served whenever you need it. I make a few of these at a time and future me is always very grateful for it!

PREP: 5 MINS
COOK: 15–20 MINS
SERVES 4

1 cup (115g) frozen chopped onions
2 tsp frozen chopped garlic
1 x 500g bag frozen sweet potato chunks
1 x 400g tin chickpeas, drained
2 x 400g tins chopped tomatoes
2 tsp smoked paprika
1 tsp dried oregano
1 tbsp frozen chopped parley
1 vegetable stock cube, crumbled

IF YOU'RE MAKING AHEAD TO *Freeze*...**SKIP TO THE BOTTOM**

IF YOU'RE COOKING *Now*... Put all the ingredients in a large pan over a medium heat and bring to the boil, stirring occasionally. Reduce the heat to a simmer, then leave to cook for 15–20 minutes, stirring occasionally, until everything is tender. Ladle into bowls and serve hot.

Zhuzh it up...

Zhuzh this one-pot dish up with a dollop of yoghurt and some thinly sliced spring onions.

IF YOU'RE MAKING AHEAD TO *Freeze*...
Simply, put all of the uncooked ingredients in a large, labelled freezer bag and freeze flat for up to 3 months.

Then... Remove the bag from the freezer and leave to defrost fully in the fridge, ideally overnight. Once defrosted, tip all the ingredients into a large pan over a medium heat and bring to the boil, stirring occasionally. Reduce the heat to a simmer, then leave to cook for 15–20 minutes, stirring occasionally, until everything is tender. Ladle into bowls and serve hot.

CHICKEN MEATBALLS

These meatballs are so versatile. I like to serve them in a sub with Arrabiata sauce (page 62) but you could also serve them over spaghetti or oven baked with a salad alongside.

PREP: 5 MINS
COOK: 25 MINS
SERVES 4

400g minced chicken
1 tsp garlic granules
2 tsp dried oregano
½ tsp salt
½ cup (23g) breadcrumbs
1 egg, beaten
olive oil, for drizzling
cooked spaghetti and Arrabbiata sauce (page 62), to serve (optional)

1   Combine all the ingredients in a large mixing bowl and use your hands to mix together well, ensuring that the herbs and breadcrumbs are evenly distributed throughout the chicken. Turn the mixture out onto a clean work surface and divide into 2 equal halves. Divide each half into 4, then each piece of meat in half again so that you have 16 equal size pieces. Roll each piece of meat into a ball with the palms of your hands.

IF YOU'RE MAKING AHEAD TO *Freeze*...**SKIP TO THE BOTTOM**

IF YOU'RE COOKING *Now*... Preheat the oven to 180°C/350°F/gas mark 4 and line a baking tray with foil. Lay the meatballs on the baking sheet and drizzle with a little oil, then transfer to the oven to cook for 20–25 minutes, until golden and cooked through. Serve hot, on a bed of pasta and dressed with Arrabiata sauce, if you like.

IF YOU'RE MAKING AHEAD TO *Freeze*...
Divide the uncooked meatballs between 2 large, labelled freezer bags and freeze flat for up to 3 months.

Then... Remove the meatballs from the freezer (if you want a half portion, just remove one of the bags) and leave to defrost fully in the fridge, ideally overnight. Once defrosted, preheat the oven to 180°C/350°F/gas mark 4 and line a baking tray with foil. Cook and serve the meatballs as described above.

MEATBALL TOAD IN THE HOLE

Deliciously herby, porky meatballs make a great substitute for sausages in this comfort-food classic. Yorkshire pudding freezes really well, making this a brilliant Sunday-lunch standby for those days when a full roast seems out of reach.

PREP: 10 MINS
COOK: 35 MINS
SERVES 4

500g minced pork (20% fat)
2 tbsp tomato purée
1 tsp dried basil
3 eggs
scant 1 cup (100g) plain flour
generous ½ cup (150ml) milk
salt and freshly ground black pepper
mashed potatoes, seasonal veg and
  gravy, to serve (optional)

1 Preheat the oven to 200°C/400°F/gas mark 6.
2 Combine the minced pork, tomato purée, dried basil, 1 of the eggs and a generous grinding of salt and pepper in a large mixing bowl. Bring the mixture together with your hands, ensuring all of the ingredients are well distributed, then form into 8 equal-sized pieces and roll into balls with the palms of your hands.
3 Spread the meatballs evenly over the base of a medium-sized baking dish, then transfer to the oven to cook for 10 minutes.
4 Meanwhile, put the flour in a large mixing bowl along with a generous grinding of salt and pepper. Make a well in the centre, then pour in the milk and crack in the 2 remaining eggs. Whisk the mixture together to make a smooth batter.
5 Remove the meatballs from the oven and make sure they are evenly spaced over the base of the baking dish, then pour the batter over the top and return to the oven for 25 minutes, until the toad in the hole is golden and beautifully risen. (You don't need to add oil to the baking dish as the hot fat from the meatballs will prevent the toad in the hole from sticking and help it to rise.)

IF YOU'RE MAKING AHEAD TO *Freeze*...**SKIP TO THE BOTTOM**

IF YOU'RE SERVING *Now*... Slice the toad in the hole into wedges and serve hot with mashed potatoes, seasonal veg and gravy alongside.

IF YOU'RE MAKING AHEAD TO *Freeze*...
Set the toad in the hole aside to cool to room temperature, then either leave whole or slice into quarters (you might want to defrost individual portions), wrap with clingfilm, label and freeze flat for up to 3 months.

Then... Remove from the freezer and leave to defrost fully in the fridge, ideally overnight. Once defrosted, preheat the oven to 180°C/350°F/gas mark 4, wrap the toad in the hole in foil and reheat for 20–25 minutes, until piping hot all the way through. Serve as described above.

MUSHROOM BOLOGNESE

This has all of the classic flavours of a Bolognese but is meat-free, so makes a great family meal for those days that you're trying to cut down on your meat intake or if you're catering for a vegetarian.

PREP: 5 MINS
COOK: 20 MINS
SERVES 4

1 tbsp vegetable or olive oil
1 cup (115g) frozen chopped onions
2 tsp frozen chopped garlic
300g white mushrooms, finely chopped
200g grated carrot
2 tsp dried oregano
2 tbsp tomato purée
2 x 400g tins chopped tomatoes
1 x 400g tin green lentils, drained
1 vegetable stock cube
salt and freshly ground black pepper
cooked spaghetti, to serve

1 Heat the oil in large pan over a medium heat, then add the onions, garlic and mushrooms and cook for 2–3 minutes, until soft and the mushrooms have released all their liquid.
2 Add the grated carrot, oregano, tomato purée, chopped tomatoes and lentils, then crumble in the stock cube and season with salt and pepper. Stir to combine, bring to the boil, then reduce to a simmer and leave to cook for 20 minutes, stirring occasionally and adding a splash of water if the mixture is too thick.
3 Remove the pan from the heat.

IF YOU'RE MAKING AHEAD TO *Freeze*...**SKIP TO THE BOTTOM**

IF YOU'RE SERVING *Now*... Ladle the Bolognese into pasta bowls over a serving of cooked spaghetti. Serve hot.

IF YOU'RE MAKING AHEAD TO *Freeze*...
Set the pan aside until the Bolognese has cooled to room temperature, then ladle into a large, labelled freezer bag and freeze flat for up to 3 months.

Then... This can be cooked from frozen or defrosted first. If defrosting, remove the bag from the freezer and leave to defrost in the fridge, ideally overnight. Once defrosted, transfer the Bolognese to a large saucepan and reheat over a medium heat, stirring occasionally, for 5–10 minutes, until piping hot. If cooking from frozen, simply tip the frozen Bolognese into a large saucepan over a low heat with a splash of water and cook, breaking up the Bolognese with a wooden spoon as it thaws, until completely defrosted and piping hot all of the way through. Serve with cooked spaghetti alongside.

SAVOURY BREAD & BUTTER PUDDING

Bread and butter pudding isn't just for dessert! This savoury version, spiked with cheese, onion and Dijon mustard, is delicious served for dinner with a fresh green salad alongside and is a brilliant way to use up the end of a loaf of slightly stale bread that would otherwise be thrown away. The mustard isn't hot, but feel free to leave it out if you'd prefer.

PREP: 10 MINS
COOK: 25–30 MINS
SERVES 4

splash of olive or vegetable oil
1 cup (115g) frozen chopped onions
2 tsp frozen chopped garlic
9 slices white bread, crusts removed
50g butter, at room temperature
2 tsp Dijon mustard
1 cup (140g) grated Cheddar cheese
3 eggs
1¼ cups (300ml) milk
generous ½ cup (150ml) double cream
salt and freshly ground black pepper
green salad leaves, to serve (optional)

1. Preheat the oven to 180°C/350°F/gas mark 4.
2. Heat the oil in a pan over a medium heat, then add the onions and garlic and cook for 2–3 minutes, until softened. Remove from the heat and set aside.
3. Spread the slices of bread with the butter, followed by a thin layer of Dijon mustard. Cut the buttered slices in half diagonally so that you have 18 buttered triangles coated in butter and Dijon mustard. Arrange half of the bread, buttered-side down and slightly overlapping, in a medium baking dish to form an even layer that covers the surface of the dish.
4. Scatter the cooked onion and garlic and half of the grated cheese over the surface of the bread, season generously with salt and pepper, then top with the remaining bread slices and sprinkle the remaining cheese over.
5. Whisk together the eggs, milk and cream in a measuring jug until combined, then pour over the bread mixture in the baking dish. Carefully transfer to the oven to bake for 25 minutes, until the surface is crisp and golden and the egg, milk and cream mixture has set.

IF YOU'RE MAKING AHEAD TO *Freeze*...**SKIP TO THE BOTTOM**

IF YOU'RE SERVING *Now*... Cut the pudding into wedges and serve hot, with a green salad alongside.

IF YOU'RE MAKING AHEAD TO *Freeze*...
Set the bread and butter pudding aside until cooled to room temperature, then cover with a lid or wrap in a layer of clingfilm followed by a layer of foil, label and freeze flat for up to 3 months.

Then... Remove the bread and butter pudding from the freezer and transfer to the fridge to fully defrost, ideally overnight. Once defrosted, preheat the oven to 180°C/350°F/gas mark 4, cover the baking dish with foil (removing any clingfilm if you used it to wrap the dish before freezing) and transfer to the oven for 20–25 minutes, until piping hot all the way through. Serve as described above.

TUNA HASH BAKE

Budget friendly, tasty and so quick to assemble, this is a brilliant dish for those days when you're rushed off your feet but still want something comforting and homemade on the table. This is a full meal in its own right, so serve as is for the ultimate fuss-free midweek dinner.

PREP: 5 MINS
COOK: 30 MINS
SERVES 4

1 tbsp olive or vegetable oil

2 cups (230g) frozen chopped onions

2 x 145g tins tuna, drained and flaked

5 spring onions, finely sliced

1 x 250g pack cherry tomatoes, halved

juice of 1 lemon

1 x 800g pack pre-made mashed potatoes

1 cup (140g) pre-grated Cheddar cheese

1 Heat the oil in a large, deep-sided frying pan over a medium heat, then add the onions and cook, stirring continuously, for 2–3 minutes, until soft.

2 Tip the cooked onions and garlic into a large mixing bowl, then add the tuna, spring onions, tomatoes and lemon juice and crumble in the mashed potatoes.

3 Give everything a mix to combine, then tip into a medium baking dish and press down in an even layer. Scatter over the grated Cheddar.

IF YOU'RE MAKING AHEAD TO *Freeze*...**SKIP TO THE BOTTOM**

IF YOU'RE COOKING *Now*... Preheat the oven to 180°C/350°F/gas mark 4, then transfer the hash to the hot oven to cook for 30 minutes, until golden. Spoon into bowls and serve hot.

IF YOU'RE MAKING AHEAD TO *Freeze*...
Cover the unbaked hash with a lid or wrap in a layer of clingfilm followed by a layer of foil, label and freeze flat for up to 3 months.

Then... This can be defrosted overnight in the fridge and cooked as above, or cooked directly from frozen. To cook from frozen, preheat the oven to 180°C/350°F/gas mark 4, cover the baking dish with foil (removing any clingfilm if you used it to wrap the dish before freezing) and transfer to the oven for 40 minutes, then remove the foil and cook for another 20 minutes, until golden.

MINCED BEEF HOTPOT

Crispy potatoes covering a layer of tasty minced beef, this is a classic winter warmer that is really economical and is sure to satisfy the hungriest of bellies. Serve it as it is or perhaps with some cauliflower cheese on the side for a really satisfying family meal.

PREP: 10 MINS
COOK: 50 MINS
SERVES 4

1 tbsp olive or vegetable oil
1 cup (115g) frozen chopped onions
2 tsp frozen chopped garlic
500g minced beef
1 cup (190g) frozen chopped carrots
1 cup (140g) frozen peas
2 tbsp tomato purée
1 tbsp dried rosemary
1 bay leaf
2 tbsp plain flour
3 cups (720ml) beef stock (use 2 stock cubes)
1 tbsp Worcestershire sauce
salt and freshly ground black pepper

On the day of serving:
2–3 medium potatoes, peeled and thinly sliced
olive oil, for drizzling

1 Heat the oil in a large, deep-sided frying pan over a medium heat, then add the onions and garlic and cook for 2–3 minutes, until softened. Add the beef to the pan and cook, breaking up with a wooden spoon as you do, until browned.

2 Add the carrots, peas, tomato purée, rosemary , bay leaf and flour to the pan and stir to combine, then add the beef stock and Worcestershire sauce and stir again. Season with salt and pepper, bring to the boil, then reduce to a simmer and leave to cook, for 20 minutes, until slightly thickened. Remove the pan from the heat.

IF YOU'RE MAKING AHEAD TO *Freeze*...**SKIP TO THE BOTTOM**

IF YOU'RE COOKING *Now*... Preheat the oven to 180°C/350°F/gas mark 4. Pour the beef mixture into a medium baking dish and arrange the sliced potatoes over the surface, overlapping them slightly to create an even layer that covers right to the edges of the dish. Drizzle with a little olive oil, then transfer to the oven to bake for 30 minutes, until the potatoes are golden and the mince is bubbling. Spoon into bowls and serve hot.

MAKE IT
Veggie!
To make this dish veggie, simply replace the beef mince with a plant-based mince and reduce the simmering time to 15 minutes.

IF YOU'RE MAKING AHEAD TO *Freeze*...
Set the pan aside until the beef mixture has cooled to room temperature, then ladle into a large, labelled freezer bag and freeze flat for up to 3 months.

Then... Remove the beef from the freezer and leave to fully defrost in the fridge, ideally overnight. Once defrosted, preheat the oven to 180°C/350°F/gas mark 4. Pour the beef mixture into a medium baking dish, then top with potatoes, bake and serve as described above.

MUSHROOM CHILLI

This is a wonderful veggie alternative to a meat-based chilli that contains all of the traditional flavours but is both meat-free and more economical to make. The mushrooms have a really meaty texture, so do give this a try even if you're catering for the most determined of carnivores.

PREP: 5 MINS
COOK: 20 MINS
SERVES 4

1 tbsp olive or vegetable oil
1 cup (115g) frozen chopped onions
2 tsp frozen chopped garlic
250g sliced mushrooms
2 cups (175g) frozen sliced peppers
1 tsp ground cumin
2 tsp smoked paprika
1 tsp chilli powder
2 x 400g tins chopped tomatoes
2 tbsp tomato purée
1 x 400g tin kidney beans, drained
juice of 1 lime
salt and freshly ground black pepper
cooked long-grain rice, to serve

1   Heat the oil in a large pan over a medium heat. Add the onions, garlic and mushrooms and cook for 2–3 minutes, stirring continuously, until soft and the mushrooms have released all their water.
2   Add the peppers, cumin, paprika, chilli powder, tinned tomatoes and tomato purée to the pan and stir to combine. Bring to the boil, then reduce the heat to a simmer and leave to cook for 15 minutes, until thickened and all of the vegetables are tender.
3   Add the kidney beans and lime juice to the pan, stir to combine and season to taste. Cook for 5 minutes more, then remove the pan from the heat.

IF YOU'RE MAKING AHEAD TO *Freeze*...**SKIP TO THE BOTTOM**

IF YOU'RE SERVING *Now*... Spoon the chilli into bowls over servings of cooked rice.

Zhuzh it up...
Serve with a dollop of yoghurt, some chopped fresh coriander and wedge of lime alongside.

IF YOU'RE MAKING AHEAD TO *Freeze*...
Set the pan aside until the chilli has cooled to room temperature, then ladle into a large, labelled freezer bag and freeze flat for up to 3 months.

Then... This can be cooked from frozen or defrosted first. If defrosting, remove the bag from the freezer and leave to defrost in the fridge, ideally overnight. Once defrosted, transfer the chilli to a large saucepan and reheat over a medium heat, stirring occasionally, for 5–10 minutes, until piping hot. If cooking from frozen, simply tip the frozen chilli into a large saucepan over a low heat with a splash of water and cook, breaking up the chilli with a wooden spoon as it thaws, until completely defrosted and piping hot all of the way through. Serve with cooked rice alongside.

VEGGIE STEW & HERBY DUMPLINGS

Dumplings are a great addition to stews as they add extra heft and fill the family up for very little cost. This winter warmer makes a perfect veggie meal, is super simple and is made in one pot, so even the washing up is easy!

PREP: 15 MINS
COOK: 40 MINS
SERVES 4

1 tbsp vegetable or olive oil
1 cup (115g) frozen chopped onions
2 tsp frozen chopped garlic
2 stalks celery, finely sliced
1 large leek, washed and roughly
  sliced
2 medium carrots, peeled and
  roughly chopped
8 baby potatoes, halved
5 large mushrooms, quartered
2 tsp dried thyme
2 tsp dried rosemary
3 cups (720ml) vegetable stock
  (use 2 stock cubes)
3 tsp cornflour
salt and freshly ground black pepper

For the dumplings:
scant 1 cup (100g) self-raising flour
½ tsp salt
50g vegetable suet
2 tsp frozen chopped parsley

1   Heat the oil in a large saucepan with a lid over a medium heat, then add the onions, garlic and celery and cook, stirring, for 4 minutes, until soft.
2   Add the leek, carrots, potatoes, mushrooms, thyme, rosemary and vegetable stock to the pan and stir to combine. Bring the mixture to the boil, then reduce the heat to a simmer and leave to cook for 15 minutes, covered with a lid, stirring occasionally.
3   While the stew is cooking, make the dumplings. Combine the flour, salt, suet and parsley in a large mixing bowl and stir to combine. Make a well in the centre and add 6 tablespoons of cold water, then use your hands to bring everything together to form a dough, adding a couple more tablespoons of water if the mixture is too dry. Once you have a smooth dough, turn out onto a lightly floured surface and cut in half, then cut each half into quarters, leaving you with 8 equal-sized pieces. Roll each piece of dough into a ball with your hands and set aside.
4   Once the stew has been simmering for 15 minutes and all the vegetables are tender, dilute the cornflour with a couple of teaspoons of water in a small bowl. Pour the cornflour slurry into the stew and stir to thicken and combine. Add salt and pepper to taste.

IF YOU'RE MAKING AHEAD TO *Freeze*...**SKIP TO THE BOTTOM**

IF YOU'RE COOKING *Now*... Remove the lid from the stew and arrange the raw dumplings over the surface, cover with the lid again and continue simmering for another 20 minutes, until the dumplings are puffed up, light and fluffy. Spoon into serving bowls and serve hot.

IF YOU'RE MAKING AHEAD TO *Freeze*...
Set the pan aside until the stew has cooled to room temperature. Ladle the stew into a large, labelled freezer bag and place the dumplings in a separate freezer bag. Freeze both flat for up to 3 months.

Then... This can be cooked directly from frozen. Preheat the oven to 180°C/350°F/gas mark 4 and line a baking sheet with foil. Lay the frozen block of stew in the base of a baking dish and arrange the frozen dumplings on the baking sheet. Cook the stew in the oven for 25 minutes, then drain off any excess water and return to the oven for another 45 minutes, adding the tray of dumplings to the oven at the same time. Ladle the stew into serving bowls and top with the dumplings. Serve hot.

PESTO & MOZZARELLA STUFFED CHICKEN

These tasty chicken breasts, oozing with herby pesto and creamy mozzarella are popular with kids and adults alike. These are great to have prepared in the freezer, as you can simply grab out as many as you need for an easy-win midweek dinner that feels fancier than it has any right to!

PREP: 5 MINS
COOK: 30–35 MINS
SERVES 4

4 skinless, boneless chicken breasts
1 ball mozzarella cheese, halved
4 tsp pesto
4 rashers bacon
roast potatoes and green beans or
  cooked pasta, to serve (optional)

1 Working with 1 chicken breast at a time, use a sharp knife to carefully slice a pocket into the thick end of each breast, being careful that your knife does not slice through the breast and puncture the other side. Repeat with the remaining 3 chicken breasts.

2 Cut each half of the mozzarella ball into 4 even slices, fill the pocket of each chicken breast with 1 teaspoon of pesto and 2 slices of mozzarella, then wrap a slice of bacon around each of the stuffed chicken breasts.

IF YOU'RE MAKING AHEAD TO *Freeze*...SKIP TO THE BOTTOM

IF YOU'RE COOKING *Now*... Preheat the oven to 180°C/350°F/gas mark 4. and line a baking sheet with foil. Lay the stuffed chicken breasts on the foil and transfer to the oven for 30–35 minutes, until the chicken is cooked through, and the filling is oozy and bubbling. Serve hot with roast potatoes and green beans or cooked pasta alongside.

IF YOU'RE MAKING AHEAD TO *Freeze*...Cut 4 squares of foil, roughly 30 x 30cm (12 x 12 inches) and place an uncooked, stuffed chicken breast in the centre of each. Bring up the edges of the foil and crimp together to seal the chicken inside. Transfer the foil-wrapped chicken breasts to a large, labelled freezer bag and freeze flat for up to 3 months.

***Then*...** Remove the chicken breasts from the freezer and leave to defrost in the fridge, ideally overnight. Once defrosted, preheat the oven to 180°C/350°F/gas mark 4 and unwrap the tops of the foil parcels to expose the chicken breasts. Lay on a baking sheet and transfer to the oven to cook for 30–35 minutes, until piping hot all the way through. Serve as described above.

SMOKY CHICKEN BURGERS

These chicken burgers are a real treat stacked with your favourite toppings and served with crispy wedges alongside. I like to spike them with a mellow undercurrent of spice, but feel free to experiment with other flavours and use what you already have to hand.

PREP: 5 MINS
COOK: 25 MINS
SERVES 4

400g minced chicken
1 tsp garlic granules
1 tsp smoked paprika
½ cup (23g) breadcrumb
½ tsp salt
1 egg, beaten

To serve:
burger buns, potato wedges and
  your choice of sauces, to serve
  (optional)

1 Put all the ingredients in a large mixing bowl and use your hands to mix together until well combined. Turn out onto a clean work surface, then divide the mixture into 4 even pieces. Using your hands, roll each piece into a ball, then press down to form a burger shape roughly the same circumference as a burger bun.

IF YOU'RE MAKING AHEAD TO *Freeze*...**SKIP TO THE BOTTOM**

IF YOU'RE COOKING *Now*... Preheat the oven to 180°C/350°F/gas mark 4 and line a baking sheet with foil. Lay the chicken burgers on the baking sheet and transfer to the oven for 25 minutes, until lightly golden and cooked all the way through. Serve the burgers in buns with your choice of sauces and potato wedges alongside.

Zhuzh it up...
Pan-fry some sliced halloumi until golden and add it to the burgers before serving.

IF YOU'RE MAKING AHEAD TO *Freeze*...
Cut 4 squares of baking paper roughly the same size of the burgers, then stack the burgers up, placing a square of parchment between each one. Transfer to a labelled freezer bag and freeze for up to 3 months.

Then... Remove as many burgers as you need from the freezer and leave to defrost in the fridge overnight. Once defrosted, preheat the oven to 180°C/350°F/gas mark 4 and line a baking sheet with foil. Remove the paper backing from the burgers and lay on the baking tray, then cook and serve as described above.

MUSHROOM DIVAN

Rich and creamy with an undercurrent of mild spice, I think of this as a veggie version of coronation chicken. If there are large appetites in your house you may want to add more mushrooms to bulk it out, but served on a bed of basmati rice, this makes a substantial meal as it is.

PREP: 5 MINS
COOK: 15 MINS
SERVES 4

1 head of broccoli, cut into florets
2 x 295g cans condensed
  mushroom soup
1 cup (240 ml) mayonnaise
200g white mushrooms, quartered
2 tsp curry powder
1 cup (175g) frozen sweetcorn
2 tsp lemon juice
cooked basmati rice, to serve

1 Bring a large pan of water to the boil, then add the broccoli florets, reduce to a simmer and leave to cook for 2 minutes, until softened but still firm.
2 While the broccoli is cooking, put the mushroom soup, mayonnaise, mushrooms, curry powder, sweetcorn and lemon juice in a large microwavable bowl and stir to combine.
3 Drain the broccoli through a colander, then add to the bowl with the other ingredients and stir to combine.

IF YOU'RE MAKING AHEAD TO *Freeze*...**SKIP TO THE BOTTOM**

IF YOU'RE COOKING *Now*... Either transfer the bowl to the microwave and cook on high for 4 minutes, until piping hot all of the way through and the vegetables are tender or tip the contents into a large pan and place over a medium heat for 15 minutes, stirring occasionally. Serve hot, spooned over a bed of cooked basmati rice.

IF YOU'RE MAKING AHEAD TO *Freeze*...
Transfer the contents of the bowl to a large, labelled freezer bag and freeze flat for up to 3 months.

Then... Remove the bag from the freezer and leave to defrost in the fridge, ideally overnight. Once defrosted either microwave the divan or heat in a pan as described above.

SWEET POTATO MISO MEDLEY

This delicious one-pot meal can be prepped ahead and ready for the freezer in a matter of moments. If you're not familiar with miso, don't be scared – it brings a delicious savoury edge to the dish that works wonderfully with the sweetness of the vegetables.

PREP: 5 MINS
COOK: 15–20 MINS
SERVES 4

1 cup (115g) frozen chopped onions
2 tsp frozen chopped garlic
1 x 500g bag frozen sweet potato chunks
1 cup (175g) frozen sliced peppers
1 x 400g tin butter beans, drained
4 tsp miso paste
1 x 400g tin coconut milk

IF YOU'RE MAKING AHEAD TO *Freeze*...SKIP TO THE BOTTOM

IF YOU'RE COOKING *Now*... Put all the ingredients in a large pan over a medium heat and stir to combine. Bring to the boil, then reduce the heat to a simmer and leave to cook, stirring occasionally, for 15 minutes, until the vegetables are tender. Spoon into serving bowls and serve hot.

IF YOU'RE MAKING AHEAD TO *Freeze*...
Tip all the ingredients into a large, labelled freezer bag, then give the contents of the bag a gentle stir to combine. Freeze flat for up to 3 months.

Then... Remove the bag from the freezer and leave to fully defrost in the fridge, ideally overnight. Once defrosted, tip the medley into a large pan over a medium heat and stir to combine. Bring to the boil, then reduce the heat to a simmer and leave to cook, stirring occasionally, for 15–20 minutes, until the vegetables are tender. Spoon into serving bowls and serve hot.

SPICED BEEF SKEWERS

These skewers are delicious wrapped in a flatbread with loads of salad, hummus and crumbled feta. They can be cooked in the oven, as below, but would also make a brilliant addition to a barbecue.

PREP: 8 MINS
COOK: 15–20 MINS
SERVES 4

500g minced beef (20% fat)
1 tsp garlic powder
1 tsp onion powder
1 tsp paprika
1 tsp ground cumin
1 tablespoon tomato purée
½ tsp salt
½ egg, beaten
freshly ground black pepper
flatbreads, hummus, feta and
  shredded lettuce, to serve
  (optional)

1 Put all the ingredients in a large bowl, using your hands to bring everything together and ensure that all of the components are well distributed.

2 Divide the mixture into 8 equal pieces, then thread each piece onto a metal or wooden skewer (roughly 18cm/7 inches long). Use your fingers to squeeze each portion of meat along its skewer into a sausage shape.

IF YOU'RE MAKING AHEAD TO *Freeze*...**SKIP TO THE BOTTOM**

IF YOU'RE COOKING *Now*... Preheat the oven to 200°C/400°F/gas mark 6 and line a baking sheet with foil. Lay the kebabs on the baking sheet and transfer to the oven to bake for 15–20 minutes, until cooked through. Once cooked, slide the kebabs off the skewers and serve with flatbreads, hummus, feta and shredded lettuce.

IF YOU'RE MAKING AHEAD TO *Freeze*...
Transfer the kofta skewers to a large, labelled freezer bag and freeze flat for up to 3 months.

Then... These can be cooked direct from frozen. Preheat the oven to 180°C/350°F/gas mark 4 and line a baking sheet with foil. Lay the kebabs on the baking sheet and transfer to the oven to bake for 25–30 minutes, until cooked through. Serve as described above.

10 *Mushroom* MEALS IN 1 HOUR

↓

YOU WILL BE MAKING

| MUSHROOM CHILLI | MUSHROOM BOLOGNESE | CREAMY MUSHROOM SOUP | GARLICKY BREADED MUSHROOMS | MUSHROOM DIVAN |

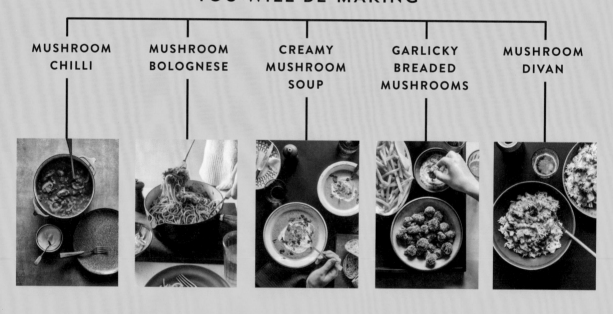

If you've got a family of carnivores but are trying to cut down on meat, mushrooms are a great place to start. Their meaty texture is a great veggie substitute, especially in dishes that would traditionally use mince. These recipes can be found elsewhere in the book but in this section they are woven together and scaled up to help you fill your freezer in one dedicated batching session. The shopping list below includes everything you will need, and I've scaled up the ingredients so you know what pack sizes to buy of each. Lay the ingredients out in piles according to the groupings under the ingredients title overleaf, then follow the numbered guide and you can't go wrong!

Shopping list

Fresh

3.4kg white mushrooms

2 x 200g bags grated carrot

2 limes

1¼ cups (300ml) double cream

2 heads broccoli

Frozen

2 x 500g packs frozen chopped onions

1 x 100g pack frozen chopped garlic

1 x 500g pack frozen sliced peppers

1 x 100g pack frozen chopped parsley

1 x 1kg pack frozen sweetcorn

Storecupboard

6 eggs

1 small bottle olive or vegetable oil

1 small bag plain flour

1 jar smoked paprika

1 jar dried oregano

1 jar ground cumin

2 x 150g packs panko breadcrumbs

6 x 400g tins chopped tomatoes

1 x 200g tube tomato purée

2 x 400g tins kidney beans

1 pack veggie stock cubes

4 x 295g cans condensed mushroom soup

1 small jar mayonnaise

1 jar curry powder

1 bottle lemon juice

1 jar garlic powder

1 jar chilli powder

2 x 400g tins cooked green lentils

INGREDIENTS

GET ORGANISED! Before you start make sure that your kitchen surfaces are cleared down, then lay all the ingredients out in individual piles according to the groupings on this page. It is also a good idea to prepare and label your freezer bags.

MUSHROOM BOLOGNESE & MUSHROOM CHILLI

1 tbsp olive or vegetable oil
4 cups (460g) frozen chopped onions
8 tsp frozen chopped garlic
1.2kg white mushrooms, roughly chopped
6 x 400g tins chopped tomatoes
1 x 200g tube tomato purée
2 x 200g bags grated carrot
4 tsp dried oregano
salt and freshly ground black pepper

For the Chilli
1 x 500g pack frozen sliced peppers
2 tsp ground cumin
4 tsp smoked paprika
2 tsp chilli powder
2 x 400g tins kidney beans, drained
2 limes, juiced

For the Bolognese
2 x 400g tins cooked green lentils, drained
2 vegetable stock cubes

CREAMY MUSHROOM SOUP

2 tbsp olive or vegetable oil
4 cups (460g) frozen chopped onions
4 tsp frozen chopped garlic
1.2kg white mushrooms
8 cups (2 litres) vegetable stock
2 tbsp frozen chopped parsley

1 cup (240ml) double cream
salt and freshly ground black pepper

GARLICKY BREADED MUSHROOMS

6 eggs, beaten
8 tbsp plain flour
3 cups (270g) panko breadcrumbs
2 tsp smoked paprika
2 tsp garlic powder
2 tsp dried oregano
2 tsp salt
600g white mushrooms
freshly ground black pepper

MUSHROOM DIVAN

2 heads broccoli
4 x 295g cans condensed mushroom soup
2 cups (480ml) mayonnaise
400g white mushrooms, quartered
4 tsp curry powder
2 cups (350g) frozen sweetcorn
4 tsp lemon juice

METHOD

MUSHROOM BOLOGNESE & MUSHROOM CHILLI

1 Heat the oil in large pan over a medium heat, then add the onions and garlic and cook for 2–3 minutes, until soft.

2 Add the mushrooms to the pan and cook for a further 8 minutes, stirring occasionally, until they are are soft and have released all of their liquid.

CREAMY MUSHROOM SOUP

3 While the mushrooms for the Bolognese and Chilli are cooking, get started on the soup. Put the mushrooms, stock and frozen parsley in a pan over a medium heat, bring to the boil then reduce to a simmer and leave to cook for 15 minutes, stirring occasionally.

MUSHROOM BOLOGNESE & CHILLI CONTINUED...

4 Drain any liquid from the mushrooms, then add the grated carrot, oregano, tomato purée and chopped tomatoes and stir to combine. Season with salt and pepper and stir again. Bring to the boil, then reduce to a simmer and cook for 15 minutes, stirring occasionally and adding a splash of water if the mixture is too thick.

GARLICKY BREADED MUSHROOMS

5 Line a large baking sheet with baking paper.

6 Set three shallow bowls on the work surface. Put the flour in the first bowl, beat the eggs into the second bowl and put the breadcrumbs, paprika, garlic powder, oregano, salt and a grinding of pepper in the third.

7 Cut any large mushrooms in half, then, dip the mushrooms first in the flour, then in the beaten egg and finally into the breadcrumbs to coat. Lay the mushrooms on the baking sheet.

8 Place the baking sheet in the freezer to freeze for 1 hour, then transfer the mushrooms to a large, labelled freezer bag and freeze for up to 3 months.

CREAMY MUSHROOM SOUP CONTINUED...

9 Once the soup has simmered for 15 minutes, remove the pan from the heat, season generously and stir through the cream. Set aside to cool while you finish making Bolognese and Chilli.

MUSHROOM BOLOGNESE CONTINUED...

10 Scoop 8 cups of the mushroom mixture from the pan into a large mixing bowl, then add the drained lentils and crumble in the stock cubes. Stir to combine, then set aside to cool to room temperature.

MUSHROOM CHILLI CONTINUED...

11 Return the pot with the remaining mushroom mixture to the stove over a medium heat, then add the sliced peppers, ground cumin, smoked paprika, chilli powder, kidney beans and lime juice and stir to combine. Bring to the boil, reduce to a simmer and leave to cook for a further 5 minutes, then remove from the heat and leave to cool to room temperature.

MUSHROOM DIVAN

12 Bring a large pan of water to the boil, then add the broccoli, reduce to a simmer and leave to cook for 2 minutes, until softened but still firm.

13 While the broccoli is cooking, put the mushroom soup, mayonnaise, mushrooms, curry powder, sweetcorn and lemon juice in a large bowl.

14 Drain the broccoli through a colander, then add to the bowl with the other ingredients and stir to combine.

15 Transfer the contents of the bowl to a large, labelled freezer bag and freeze flat for up to 3 months.

CREAMY MUSHROOM SOUP CONTINUED...

16 When the soup has cooled, use a hand blender to blitz until smooth.

17 Divide the soup between 2 large, labelled freezer bags and freeze flat for up to 3 months.

MUSHROOM BOLOGNESE CONTINUED...

18 Once cooled, divide the Bolognese mixture between 2 large, labelled freezer bags and freeze flat for up to 3 months.

MUSHROOM CHILLI CONTINUED...

19 Once cooled, divide the chilli mixture between 2 large, labelled freezer bags and freeze flat for up to 3 months.

Congratulations
You now have 10 evening meals ready for the freezer!

WHEN YOU COME TO COOK

MUSHROOM CHILLI

This can be cooked from frozen or defrosted first. If defrosting, remove the bag from the freezer and leave to defrost in the fridge, ideally overnight. Once defrosted, transfer the chilli to a large saucepan and reheat over a medium heat, stirring occasionally, for 5–10 minutes, until piping hot. If cooking from frozen, simply tip the frozen chilli into a large saucepan over a low heat with a splash of water and cook, breaking up the chilli with a wooden spoon as it thaws, until completely defrosted and piping hot all the way through. Serve with cooked rice alongside.

MUSHROOM BOLOGNESE

This can be cooked from frozen or defrosted first. If defrosting, remove the bag from the freezer and leave to defrost in the fridge, ideally overnight. Once defrosted, transfer the Bolognese to a large saucepan and reheat over a medium heat, stirring occasionally, for 5–10 minutes, until piping hot. If cooking from frozen, simply tip the frozen Bolognese into a large saucepan over a low heat with a splash of water and cook, breaking up the Bolognese with a wooden spoon as it thaws, until completely defrosted and piping hot all the way through. Serve with cooked spaghetti alongside.

CREAMY MUSHROOM SOUP

The day before you want to serve the soup, remove it from the freezer and place it in the fridge overnight to defrost. The next day, pour the soup into a large pan and place over medium-low heat until piping hot all the way through.

GARLICKY BREADED MUSHROOMS

Lay the frozen mushrooms on a baking paper-lined baking sheet and drizzle with a little oil. Transfer to an oven preheated to 200°C/400°F/gas mark 6 and cook for 20–25 minutes, until golden and piping hot all the way through. Serve with the aioli on page 58, if you like.

MUSHROOM DIVAN

Remove the bag from the freezer and leave to defrost in the fridge, ideally overnight. Once defrosted either microwave on high for 4 minutes, until piping hot all the way through and the vegetables are tender, or tip the contents into a large pan and place over a medium heat for 15 minutes, stirring occasionally. Serve hot, spooned over a bed of cooked basmati rice.

FAKEAWAYS

BUTTER CHICKEN

PREP: 10 MINS
COOK: 25 MINS
SERVES: 4

1 tbsp butter
1 cup (115g) frozen chopped onions
2 tsp frozen chopped garlic
2 tsp frozen chopped ginger
2 tsp frozen chopped chilli
4 skinless, boneless chicken
   breasts, cut into bite-sized pieces
2 tsp garam masala
2 tsp ground cumin
2 tbsp tomato purée
1 x 400g can chopped tomatoes
½ cup (120ml) chicken stock
½ cup (120ml) double cream
cooked basmati rice, poppadoms
   and mango chutney, to serve

1   Melt the butter in a large pan over a medium heat, then add the onions, garlic, ginger, chilli and chopped chicken and cook, stirring, for 4–5 minutes, until the chicken is sealed and the onions are soft and translucent.

2   Add the garam masala, ground cumin, tomato purée, chopped tomatoes, chicken stock and cream and stir to combine. Bring the mixture to a boil, then reduce to a simmer and leave to cook, stirring occasionally, for 25 minutes. Remove from the heat.

IF YOU'RE MAKING AHEAD TO *Freeze*...**SKIP TO THE BOTTOM**

IF YOU'RE SERVING *Now*... Spoon the curry into bowls over a bed of cooked basmati rice and serve hot, with mango chutney and poppadoms alongside.

MAKE IT
Veggie!

Substitute the chicken for 500g of frozen sweet potato chunks and reduce the simmering time to 20 minutes for a delicious veggie alternative.

IF YOU'RE MAKING AHEAD TO *Freeze*...
Leave the butter chicken to cool to room temperature, then transfer to a large, labelled freezer bag and freeze flat for up to 3 months.

Then... This can be cooked from frozen or defrosted first. If defrosting, remove the bag from the freezer and leave to defrost in the fridge, ideally overnight. Once defrosted, transfer the butter chicken to a large saucepan and reheat over a medium heat, stirring occasionally, for 5–10 minutes, until piping hot. If cooking from frozen, simply tip the frozen butter chicken into a large saucepan over a low heat with a splash of water and cook, breaking up the curry with a wooden spoon as it thaws, until completely defrosted and piping hot all of the way through. Serve with cooked basmati rice alongside.

CHICKEN DHANSAK

PREP: 10 MINS
COOK: 35 MINS
SERVES 4

1 tbsp vegetable oil
1 cup (115g) frozen chopped onions
2 tsp frozen chopped garlic
2 tsp frozen chopped ginger
4–6 skinless, boneless chicken
   thighs, cut into bite-sized pieces
2 tbsp mild curry powder
1 tsp ground coriander
½ tsp chilli powder (optional)
2 x 400g tins chopped tomatoes
1 ⅔ cups (400ml) chicken stock
½ cup (100g) red lentils
1 tbsp frozen chopped coriander
cooked basmati rice and natural
   yoghurt, to serve (optional)

1 Heat the oil in a large, high-sided frying pan over a medium heat, then add the onions, garlic and ginger and cook for 2–3 minutes, stirring continuously, until soft.
2 Add the chicken to the pan and cook, stirring continuously, until sealed, then add the curry powder, ground coriander and chilli powder, if using, and stir to coat the chicken.
3 Add the chopped tomatoes, chicken stock and lentils to the pan and stir to combine. Bring the mixture to the boil, then reduce the heat to a simmer and leave to cook, loosely covered, for around 35 minutes, stirring occasionally, until the sauce has thickened and the lentils are tender.
4 Stir through the chopped coriander and remove the pan from the heat.

IF YOU'RE MAKING AHEAD TO *Freeze*...SKIP TO THE BOTTOM

IF YOU'RE SERVING *Now...* Spoon the dhansak into serving bowls and serve with basmati rice and natural yoghurt for spooning over alongside, if you like.

MAKE IT
Veggie!
Substitute the chicken thighs with one large diced sweet potato and cook in the same way.

IF YOU'RE MAKING AHEAD TO *Freeze*...
Leave the dhansak to cool to room temperature, then transfer to a large, labelled freezer bag and freeze flat for up to 3 months.

Then... This can be cooked from frozen or defrosted first. If defrosting, remove the bag from the freezer and leave to defrost in the fridge, ideally overnight. Once defrosted, transfer the dhansak to a large saucepan and reheat over a medium heat, stirring occasionally, for 5–10 minutes, until piping hot. If cooking from frozen, simply tip the frozen dhansak into a large saucepan over a low heat with a splash of water and cook, breaking up the curry with a wooden spoon as it thaws, until completely defrosted and piping hot all of the way through. Serve with cooked basmati rice alongside.

CAULIFLOWER & CHICKPEA MADRAS

This delicious vegan curry adds a much-needed injection of veg to a home curry night and will be a hit with even the most committed meat eater. For speed and to keep cost down, I've used a ready-made curry paste here, which makes it easy to adjust the spice level to your family's taste.

PREP: 10 MINS
COOK: 15 MINS
SERVES 4

1 large cauliflower, cut into florets
1 tbsp oil
1 cup (115g) frozen chopped onions
1 tsp frozen chopped garlic
1 tsp frozen chopped ginger
1–2 tbsp madras curry paste
  (I like Patak's)
2 tbsp tomato purée
2 x 400g cans chopped tomatoes
1 x 400g can chickpeas, drained
cooked basmati rice, naan breads
  and poppadoms, to serve
  (optional)

1 Bring a large pan of water to the boil over a medium heat, then add the cauliflower florets and cook for 4 minutes, until partially cooked. Drain and set aside.

2 Heat the oil in a large frying pan over a medium heat, then add the onions, garlic and ginger and cook for 2–3 minutes, stirring continuously, until softened.

3 Add the madras paste, tomato purée, part-cooked cauliflower, chopped tomatoes and drained chickpeas to the pan and stir to combine. Bring the mixture to a boil, then reduce to a simmer and leave to cook, stirring occasionally, for 15 minutes, until thickened. Add a splash of water to the pan if the sauce is too thick or starts to stick. Remove from the heat.

IF YOU'RE MAKING AHEAD TO *Freeze*...**SKIP TO THE BOTTOM**

IF YOU'RE SERVING *Now*... Spoon the curry into bowls over a bed of cooked basmati rice and serve hot, with naan breads and poppadoms alongside, if you like.

IF YOU'RE MAKING AHEAD TO *Freeze*...
Leave the madras to cool to room temperature, then transfer to a large, labelled freezer bag and freeze flat for up to 3 months.

Then... This can be cooked from frozen or defrosted first. If defrosting, remove the bag from the freezer and leave to defrost in the fridge, ideally overnight. Once defrosted, transfer the madras to a large saucepan and reheat over a medium heat, stirring occasionally, for 5–10 minutes, until piping hot. If cooking from frozen, simply tip the frozen madras into a large saucepan over a low heat with a splash of water and cook, breaking up the curry with a wooden spoon as it thaws, until completely defrosted and piping hot all of the way through. Serve with cooked basmati rice alongside.

GIANT VEGAN SAMOSAS

PREP: 15 MINS
COOK: 25 MINS
SERVES 4

2 medium white potatoes, peeled and cut into 1cm (½ inch) cubes

1 carrot, peeled and cut into 1cm (½ inch) cubes

9 tbsp vegetable oil

1 cup (115g) frozen chopped onions

2 tsp frozen chopped garlic

1 cup (155g) frozen peas

3 tsp mild curry powder

1 tsp ground cumin

1 tsp turmeric

1 pack filo pastry

mango chutney, to serve

1 Preheat the oven to 180°C/350°F/gas mark 4.

2 Put the potatoes and carrots in a pan and cover with cold water. Place over a high heat and bring to the boil, then reduce to a simmer and leave to cook until very soft, this will take around 15 minutes.

3 Meanwhile, heat 1 tablespoon of the oil in a large frying pan over a medium heat, then add the onions, garlic and peas and cook, stirring continuously, for 5–6 minutes. Add the curry powder, cumin and turmeric and cook for an additional minute, then remove the pan from the heat and tip the contents into a large mixing bowl.

4 Drain the potatoes and carrots then add to the mixing bowl with the other vegetables. Using a fork, roughly mash the potatoes and carrots into the other veg and stir to combine. Set aside to cool.

6 Lay a sheet of filo pastry flat on your worktop then brush it all over with the some of the remaining oil. Top with another sheet of filo, brush with oil again, then repeat with a third sheet of filo.

7 Spoon a quarter of the filling into the top left quadrant of the oiled filo, then bring up the bottom edge of the filo sheets to meet the top and enclose the filling. Now fold the top left corner (with the filling) in and over so that you have one diagonal edge. Fold again to create a triangle shape, continuing to fold and tuck until you have a neat samosa. (Don't worry if you don't get it first time – it takes practice!)

8 Repeat the layering, oiling, filling and folding steps above until you have 4 large samosas.

IF YOU'RE MAKING AHEAD TO *Freeze*...SKIP TO THE BOTTOM

IF YOU'RE COOKING *Now*... Preheat the oven to 180°C/350°F/gas mark 4 and line a baking sheet. Transfer the samosas to the oven to bake for 25 minutes, until crisp and golden. Serve hot with mango chutney alongside for dipping.

IF YOU'RE MAKING AHEAD TO *Freeze*...
Wrap each of the samosas neatly in foil, then transfer to a large labelled freezer bag and freeze flat for up to 3 months.

Then... These can be cooked straight from frozen. Remove from the freezer, carefully unwrap the samosas and brush all over with a little vegetable oil, then rewrap in foil and place on a lined baking sheet. Bake in an oven preheated to 180°C/350°F/gas mark 4 for 25 minutes, then remove the foil and return to the oven for an additional 10 minutes, until crisp, golden and piping hot all the way through.

BEEF KEEMA

Keema is a great option when you fancy a curry in a hurry but want to keep the cost down. Mince cooks quickly, takes on flavour brilliantly and is one of the most economical ways of purchasing meat.

PREP: 5 MINS
COOK: 20 MINS
SERVES 4

1 tbsp vegetable oil
1 cup (115g) frozen chopped onions
2 tsp frozen diced garlic
2 tsp frozen diced ginger
500g minced beef
2 tbsp medium curry powder
2 x 400g tins chopped tomatoes
½ cup (120ml) beef stock (use 1 stock cube)
1 cup (140g) frozen peas
cooked basmati rice, to serve

1 Heat the oil in a large saucepan over a medium heat, then add the onions, garlic and ginger and cook, stirring, for 2–3 minutes until the onions are soft and translucent.

2 Add the minced beef to the pan and cook, stirring continuously, for 5 minutes, until browned, then stir through the curry powder, chopped tomatoes, beef stock and peas. Bring the mixture to the boil, then reduce the heat to a simmer and leave to cook, stirring occasionally, for 20 minutes. Remove from the heat.

IF YOU'RE MAKING AHEAD TO *Freeze*...SKIP TO THE BOTTOM

IF YOU'RE SERVING *Now*... Spoon the keema into serving bowls and serve with basmati rice alongside.

MAKE IT
Veggie!
Substitute the beef mince with plant-based mince and reduce the cooking time at the end of step 2 to 15 minutes.

IF YOU'RE MAKING AHEAD TO *Freeze*...
Leave the keema to cool to room temperature, then transfer to a large, labelled freezer bag and freeze flat for up to 3 months.

Then... This can be cooked from frozen or defrosted first. If defrosting, remove the bag from the freezer and leave to defrost in the fridge, ideally overnight. Once defrosted, transfer the keema to a large saucepan and reheat over a medium heat, stirring occasionally, for 5–10 minutes, until piping hot. If cooking from frozen, simply tip the frozen keema into a large saucepan over a low heat with a splash of water and cook, breaking up the keema with a wooden spoon as it thaws, until completely defrosted and piping hot all of the way through. Serve with cooked basmati rice alongside.

MEXICAN BEEF NACHO TOPPER

Cheesy, spicy and loaded with flavour, this is the ultimate sharing dish for informal entertaining when you have lots of hungry mouths to feed. If you're feeding more than 4 people, this is easy to scale up by simply doubling or tripling the ingredient amounts.

PREP: 10 MINS
COOK: 8–10 MINS
SERVES 4

splash of vegetable or olive oil
1 cup (115g) frozen chopped onions
1 tsp frozen chopped garlic
250g minced beef
1 x 30g packet taco seasoning
1 x 395g tin mixed beans in chilli sauce
2 tbsp tomato purée
1 cup (175g) frozen sliced peppers

To serve:
1 x 200g bag lightly salted tortilla chips
1 cup (90g) pre-grated Cheddar cheese

1 Heat a splash of oil in a large pan over a medium heat, then add the onions, garlic and beef mince and cook, stirring, for about 5 minutes, until the onions are translucent and the meat has browned.
2 Drain any excess fat from the pan, then return to the heat and add the taco seasoning, beans in chilli sauce, tomato purée and sliced peppers. Give everything another stir to combine, bring to the boil, then reduce to a simmer and leave to cook, stirring occasionally, for 5 minutes. Remove from the heat.

IF YOU'RE MAKING AHEAD TO *Freeze*...**SKIP TO THE BOTTOM**

IF YOU'RE SERVING *Now*... Preheat the oven to 180°C/350°F/gas mark 4. Transfer the tortilla chips to a large baking dish and warm in the oven for 5 minutes, until crisp. Remove from the oven and ladle the beef chilli over the top of the dish. Scatter over the grated cheese then return the dish to the oven for 6–8 minutes, until the cheese is melted and bubbling. Put the dish in the middle of the table for everyone to enjoy.

MAKE IT *Veggie!*
Simply replace the minced beef with a plant-based mince of your choice and cook in the exact same way.

Zhuzh it up...
Scatter over some fresh coriander and serve with guacamole and pickled jalapenos alongside.

IF YOU'RE MAKING AHEAD TO *Freeze*...
Leave the beef chilli to cool to room temperature, then transfer to a large, labelled freezer bag and freeze flat for up to 3 months.

Then... Remove the bag from the freezer and leave to defrost in the fridge, ideally overnight. Once defrosted, tip the beef chilli into a large saucepan over a medium heat and reheat, stirring occasionally, for 5–10 minutes, until piping hot. While the chilli is reheating, warm the tortilla chips then assemble the Mexican Nacho Topper as described above.

BFC CORNFLAKE CHICKEN

The secret to this brilliant chicken is the coating of cornflakes, which gives a brilliant crunch without any deep frying – making this not only more economical, but healthier than the traditional fast-food version, too. Win win!

PREP: 10 MINS
COOK: 25 MINS
SERVES 4

3 cups (105g) cornflakes
1 tsp garlic granules
1 tsp smoked paprika
½ tsp salt
2 eggs, beaten
4 skinless, boneless chicken
  breasts, each cut into 3–4
  goujons
oil, for drizzling

1 Line a baking sheet with foil.
2 Put the cornflakes in a large freezer bag and bash with a rolling pin to make fine crumbs. Transfer the cornflake crumbs to a shallow bowl along with the garlic granules, smoked paprika and salt, and stir to combine. Set another bowl next to the first and add the beaten eggs.
3 Working with one piece at a time, dip the chicken first in the egg then in the breadcrumbs, ensuring that it is well coated in both. Lay the coated chicken on the prepared baking sheet and repeat with the remaining pieces.

IF YOU'RE MAKING AHEAD TO *Freeze*...**SKIP TO THE BOTTOM**

IF YOU'RE COOKING *Now*... Preheat the oven to 180°C/350°F/gas mark 4. Once the oven is hot, drizzle the goujons with a little oil then transfer the baking sheet to the oven and leave to cook for 20–25 minutes, until golden and cooked through. Serve hot with chips alongside, if you like.

Zhuzh it up...
If you like a bit more spice, add more paprika to the cornflake mixture when breading the chicken.

IF YOU'RE MAKING AHEAD TO *Freeze*...
Transfer the entire baking sheet to the freezer for 1 hour to allow the chicken pieces to firm up. Once part frozen, transfer the chicken to a large, labelled freezer bag and freeze flat for up to 3 months.

Then... The chicken can be cooked directly from frozen. Preheat the oven to 180°C/350°F/gas mark 4 and line a baking sheet with baking paper. Transfer the frozen chicken pieces to the prepared baking sheet in a single layer, drizzle over a little oil then cook in the oven for 20–25 minutes, until crisp, golden and piping hot all of the way through.

BREADED HALLOUMI FRIES

What more could you want than hot, melty cheese in a coating of crunchy breadcrumbs? These halloumi fries are crispy, delicious and make the perfect weekend treat to enjoy in front of the telly. Watch out though - they are addictive!

PREP: 10 MINS
COOK: 15–20 MINS
SERVES 4

8 tbsp plain flour
2 eggs, beaten
2 cups (90g) panko breadcrumbs
1 tsp garlic powder
1 tsp smoked paprika
2 x 225g blocks halloumi, each
  block cut into 6–8 batons
salt and freshly ground black pepper
oil, for drizzling

1 Set 3 shallow bowls next to each other on the kitchen counter and line a baking sheet with baking paper.
2 Put the flour in the first bowl along with a generous grinding of salt and pepper, the eggs in the second bowl, and the breadcrumbs, garlic powder and paprika in the third bowl.
3 Working with 1 piece of halloumi at a time, dip the halloumi batons first in the flour, then in the egg, then in breadcrumbs, ensuring that each piece of halloumi is well coated in each bowl. Lay the breaded halloumi fries on the prepared baking sheet.

IF YOU'RE MAKING AHEAD TO *Freeze*...**SKIP TO THE BOTTOM**

IF YOU'RE COOKING *Now...* Preheat the oven to 180°C/350°F/gas mark 4. Drizzle the halloumi fries with a little oil then transfer to the oven for 15–20 minutes, until crisp and golden.

Zhuzh it up...

Serve these with a drizzle of hot sauce (I like Frank's!) for a spicy treat!

IF YOU'RE MAKING AHEAD TO *Freeze*...
Put the baking sheet in the freezer for 1 hour to allow the halloumi fries to firm up, then transfer to a labelled freezer bag and freeze flat for up to 3 months.

Then... The halloumi fries can be cooked directly from frozen. Preheat the oven to 180°C/350°F/gas mark 4 and line a baking sheet with baking paper. Transfer the frozen halloumi fries to the prepared baking sheet in a single layer, then cook in the oven for 20–25 minutes, until crisp, golden and piping hot all of the way through.

CHIP SHOP FISH

The ultimate chip shop fish! This is so much cheaper than buying battered fish from the chippy and amazingly easy to make at home. Frying fish can leave your clothes and house a bit smelly, so this is the perfect recipe to batch in advance. Simply grab from the freezer and throw in the oven for the ultimate easy weekend treat.

PREP: 10 MINS
COOK: 3-5 MINS
SERVES 4

2¾ cups (300g) plain flour
3 tsp baking powder
1 tsp salt
410ml cold water
4 fillets white fish (coley, pollock, cod or haddock work well), not too thick
500ml vegetable oil

1   Put the oil in a deep-fat fryer or large, deep-sided saucepan and heat slowly until the oil reaches 180°C/350°F. If you aren't using a deep-fat fryer and don't have an instant-read thermometer carefully add a spoonful of the batter (see below) to the pan – if it floats and turns golden brown within 60 seconds then the oil is ready. If the batter burns then the oil is too hot and should be carefully removed from the heat to cool down.

2   While the oil is heating, combine the flour, baking powder and salt in a large mixing bowl, then slowly pour in the water, whisking continuously to a smooth batter as you do.

3   Pat the fish fillets dry on kitchen paper, then working with a single fillet at a time, dip the fish in the batter until fully coated and carefully transfer to the hot oil. Cook the fish in 2 batches for 3–5 minutes each, until the batter is crisp and golden and the fish is cooked through. Remove the fish from the oil and leave to drain on kitchen paper while you cook the second batch.

IF YOU'RE MAKING AHEAD TO *Freeze*...**SKIP TO THE BOTTOM**

IF YOU'RE SERVING *Now*... The fish is now ready to be served with chip-shop chips and mushy peas alongside (see opposite).

IF YOU'RE MAKING AHEAD TO *Freeze*...
Leave the fish to cool to room temperature, then lay on a lined baking sheet and freeze for 1 hour to firm up. Once part-frozen, transfer the fish to a large, labelled freezer bag and freeze flat for up to 3 months.

Then... These can be cooked directly from frozen. Simply preheat the oven to 180°C/350°F/gas mark 4 and line a baking sheet with foil. Lay the frozen fish on the prepared baking sheet and transfer to the oven for 25–30 minutes, until crisp, golden and piping hot all of the way through. Serve as described above.

CHIP-SHOP CHIPS

PREP: 10 MINS **COOK:** 30–40 MINS **SERVES** 4

6 large Maris Piper
    potatoes, peeled and cut
    into chips

1 tbsp plain flour
4 tbsp vegetable oil
salt

1   Line a baking sheet with foil. Put the chipped
    potatoes in a large saucepan and cover with cold
    water. Put over a high heat until the water comes
    to a boil, then reduce to a simmer and cook for 5
    minutes. Strain through a colander then return the
    chips to the pan over the heat for a minute or so,
    moving the pan as you do to stop them from sticking,
    to dry the chips out.

2   Remove the pan from the heat, add the flour and toss
    gently to coat, then add the oil to the pan and toss
    again. Season with salt, then tip the chips onto the
    prepared baking sheet and spread out in an even layer.

IF YOU'RE MAKING AHEAD TO *Freeze*...SKIP TO
THE BOTTOM

IF YOU'RE COOKING *Now*... Preheat the oven to
200°C/400°F/gas mark 6. Transfer the baking sheet to
the oven and cook for 30–40 minutes, until the chips are
crisp and golden. Serve hot.

IF YOU'RE MAKING AHEAD TO *Freeze*...Transfer
the baking sheet to the freezer for 1 hour to allow
the chips to firm up, then transfer to a large, labelled
freezer bag and freeze flat for up to 3 months.

Then... Preheat the oven to 200°C/400°F/gas
mark 6 and line a baking sheet with foil. Transfer
the chips to the prepared baking sheet in an even
layer, then cook in the oven for 40–50 minutes,
until crisp and golden.

PEA SMASH

PREP: 5 MINS **COOK:** 5 MINS **SERVES** 4

1½ cups (225g) frozen
    peas
knob of butter

1 tsp dried mint
salt and freshly ground
    black pepper

1   Cook the peas in a pan of boiling water for 3 minutes.
    Drain through a colander and transfer to a bowl. Add
    the butter, mint and some salt and pepper to the bowl,
    then mash with a masher to your desired consistency.

IF YOU'RE MAKING AHEAD TO *Freeze*...SKIP TO
THE BOTTOM

IF YOU'RE SERVING *Now*... The peas are now ready to
serve.

IF YOU'RE MAKING AHEAD TO *Freeze*...Leave
peas to cool to room temperature, then transfer to a
labelled freezer bag and freeze flat for up to 3 months.

Then... Remove the bag of peas from the freezer
and leave to defrost in the fridge, ideally overnight.
Once defrosted, the peas can be transferred to a
heatproof bowl and reheated in the microwave until
piping hot.

SHARING SHISH KEBAB

This is a brilliant meal to serve in the middle of the table and let everyone dig in. I love this kind of informal feasting, where everyone is leaning over each other and passing things around – it immediately makes any meal feel relaxed and fun.

PREP: 10 MINS
COOK: 12–14 MINS
SERVES 4

2 tbsp tomato purée
2 tsp smoked paprika
3 tsp frozen chopped garlic
1 tbsp dried oregano
juice of 1 lemon
½ cup (100g) natural yoghurt
1 tsp salt
8 skinless, boneless chicken thighs
freshly ground black pepper

To serve:
flatbreads
chilli sauce
shredded lettuce
natural yoghurt

1   Put the tomato purée, smoked paprika, frozen garlic, oregano, lemon juice and natural yoghurt in a large mixing bowl and stir to combine. Add the salt and a generous grinding of pepper and mix again.

IF YOU'RE MAKING AHEAD TO *Freeze*...**SKIP TO THE BOTTOM**

IF YOU'RE SERVING *Now*... Preheat the grill to medium and line a grill pan with foil. Add the chicken to the bowl and use your hands to give everything a mix and ensure the chicken is well coated. Thread the chicken thighs onto two large skewers so that each skewer runs parallel to the other through all the pieces of chicken (if you are using wooden skewers, it's a good idea to soak them in cold water for half an hour or so before using). Try and position the skewers to the outer edges of the chicken, rather than closely together in the middle. Lay the skewered chicken on the prepared grill pan and cook under the grill for 12–14 minutes on each side, until juicy, golden brown and cooked all the way through. Remove the skewers from the chicken and carve the kebab into slices, then place in the middle of the table with your chosen accompaniments and let everyone dig in!

Half & Half

To reduce the cost further and cut down the amount of meat used in this dish, reduce the amount of chicken to 4 thighs and intersperse the chicken with thickly sliced peppers on the skewer.

IF YOU'RE MAKING AHEAD TO *Freeze*...Transfer the marinade to a large, labelled freezer bag along with the chicken, then give the bag a squeeze to ensure that the chicken is well coated in the marinade. Freeze flat for up to 3 months.

Then... Remove the bag from the freezer and leave to defrost in the fridge, ideally overnight. Once defrosted, thread the chicken onto skewers, cook and serve as described above.

SLOW-COOKED THAI BEEF CURRY

I love my slow cooker! Throw in a few ingredients in the morning and come dinner time they have been transformed into something truly delicious. This Thai curry is no exception and will have leave house fragrant with the delicious aromas of Thailand as it bubbles away.

PREP: 5 MINS
COOK: 3–6 HOURS (DEPENDING ON SLOW COOKER SETTING)
SERVES 4

600g beef brisket chunks
2–3 tbsp Thai green curry paste
1 cup (115g) frozen chopped onions
2 tsp frozen chopped garlic
2 cups (350g) frozen sliced
  peppers
1 x 400g can coconut milk
4 tbsp soy sauce

On the day:
220g green beans, trimmed
2 tbsp frozen chopped coriander
juice of 1 lime
cooked jasmine rice, to serve

IF YOU'RE MAKING AHEAD TO *Freeze*...SKIP TO THE BOTTOM

IF YOU'RE SERVING *Now*... Put the beef brisket, Thai curry paste, onions, garlic, peppers, coconut milk and soy sauce in the slow cooker and stir to combine. Turn on the slow cooker and leave to cook for 3 hours on high, or 6 hours on low. 30 minutes before the end of the cooking time, add the green beans, coriander and lime juice. Serve hot with jasmine rice alongside.

Half & Half

To bring the cost down even further and reduce your meat intake, reduce the beef brisket to 300g and add 300g of cooked, halved new potatoes to the curry before serving.

IF YOU'RE MAKING AHEAD TO *Freeze*...Put the beef brisket, Thai curry paste, onions, garlic, peppers, coconut milk and soy sauce in a large, labelled freezer bag and freeze flat for up to 3 months.

Then... Remove the bag from the freezer and leave to defrost in the fridge, ideally overnight. Once defrosted, tip the ingredients into the slow cooker and cook and serve as described above.

BATCH BURGER

These are my take on everyone's favourite fast-food treat at home! Everyone loves a burger from time to time, and piled high with lettuce and pickles and paired with my burger sauce and coleslaw recipes (opposite), these are better than anything you can get at a drive-through and far kinder on the wallet!

PREP: 10 MINS
COOK: 8–10 MINS
MAKES 8 BURGERS

450g minced beef (15–20% fat)
salt and freshly ground black pepper

To serve:
burger buns
shredded lettuce
pickles
burger sauce (opposite)
coleslaw (opposite)
oven French fries

1 Put the minced beef in a large mixing bowl and season generously with salt and pepper. Using your hands, combine the beef and seasoning until well mixed through.

2 Divide the beef into 8 equal-sized pieces. Roll each piece of beef into a ball then press down to form a flat round roughly the circumference of a burger bun.

IF YOU'RE MAKING AHEAD TO *Freeze*...**SKIP TO THE BOTTOM**

IF YOU'RE COOKING *Now*... Heat a dry frying pan over a medium heat, then add the burgers in batches of 2 or 3 at a time and cook for 2 minutes on each side, until cooked through. Set aside while you cook the remaining burgers. Layer the burgers up in buns with the shredded lettuce, pickles and burger sauce, and serve with French fries and coleslaw alongside.

IF YOU'RE MAKING AHEAD TO *Freeze*...
Cut 8 squares of baking paper and lay a burger on each. Make 2 stacks of 4 burgers, then freeze each stack in a separate, labelled freezer bag for up to 3 months.

Then... These can be cooked directly from frozen. Simply remove the required amount of burgers from the freezer and peel off their baking paper backing. Heat a dry frying pan over a medium heat, then add the burgers in batches of 2 or 3 at a time and cook for 3 minutes on each side, until cooked through. Set aside while you cook the remaining burgers. Layer up and serve the burgers as described above.

BURGER SAUCE & COLESLAW

These recipes aren't suitable for the freezer, but can be whipped up in a flash to serve alongside your burgers. The sauce is actually the base for the coleslaw and, once made, will keep in a sealed jar in the fridge for up to 3 weeks. A full quantity of burger sauce will make enough for 4 burgers and the coleslaw, feeding a family of 4.

PREP: 10 MINS
SERVES 4

For the burger sauce:
½ cup (120ml) mayonnaise
3 tbsp tomato ketchup
1 tbsp American mustard
5 small gherkins, finely diced
salt and freshly ground black pepper

For the coleslaw:
½ small white cabbage, finely sliced
1 red onion, finely sliced
1 large carrot, peeled and grated
½ quantity burger sauce (above)
salt and freshly ground black pepper

1 To make the burger sauce, simply combine all of the ingredients in a jar or bowl, season generously and mix well to combine.
2 To make the coleslaw, combine the prepared vegetables with the burger sauce and stir to combine. Taste and add seasoning if necessary. The coleslaw is best served on the day it is made but will keep in the fridge for a couple of days.

SWEET & SOUR CHICKEN BALLS

This is the kind of thing many people love to order at a takeaway but would never think of making at home. This version is actually really easy, delicious and far cheaper than buying them from a restaurant could ever be!

PREP: 15 MINS
COOK: 20 MINS
SERVES 4

3 skinless, boneless chicken breasts
150g plain flour
2 tsp baking powder
180ml cold water
3 cups (720ml) vegetable oil, for frying
salt and freshly ground black pepper

To serve:
1 jar store-bought sweet & sour sauce
egg-fried rice and prawn crackers (optional)

1 Using a sharp knife, slice each of the chicken breasts into 8 equal slices, Season the chicken generously with salt and pepper, then set aside.

2 Put the flour and baking powder in a large mixing bowl, then slowly whisk in 180ml of cold water to make a smooth batter.

3 Put the oil in a deep-fat fryer or large, deep-sided saucepan and heat slowly until the oil reaches 180°C/350°F. If you're not using a deep-fat fryer and don't have an instant-read thermometer carefully add a spoonful of the batter to the pan – if it floats and turns golden brown within 60 seconds then the oil is ready. If the batter burns then the oil is too hot and should be carefully removed from the heat to cool down.

4 Dip the chicken pieces in the batter, shake off any excess, then transfer to the hot oil. I do this in batches of 6 at a time to ensure that I know how long everything has been cooking. Cook the chicken for 5 minutes, turning halfway through, until the batter is crisp and golden brown, then remove from the oil and set aside to drain on kitchen paper. Repeat until all of the chicken has been cooked.

IF YOU'RE MAKING AHEAD TO *Freeze*...SKIP TO THE BOTTOM

IF YOU'RE SERVING *Now*... Warm the sweet and sour sauce over a gentle heat in a small pan, until piping hot. Serve the chicken balls with the sweet and sour sauce drizzled over and egg-fried rice and prawn crackers alongside, if you like.

IF YOU'RE MAKING AHEAD TO *Freeze*...
Leave the chicken to cool to room temperature, then transfer to a large, labelled freezer bag and freeze flat for up to 3 months.

Then... Remove the bag from the freezer and leave to defrost in the fridge, ideally overnight. Once defrosted, preheat the oven to 180°C/350°F/gas mark 4 and line a baking sheet with foil. Lay the chicken balls on the baking sheet and transfer to the oven for 15–20 minutes, until piping hot all of the way through. Heat the sweet and sour sauce and serve the chicken balls as described above.

SALMON ENCHILADAS

Tinned salmon is a really economical storecupboard staple that is so versatile. Here it gets the Mexican treatment with the addition of fiery chipotle paste, baked into delicious enchiladas.

PREP: 10 MINS
COOK: 20 MINS
SERVES 4

1 tbsp olive or vegetable oil
1 cup (115g) frozen diced onions
2 tsp frozen chopped garlic
1 cup (175g) frozen sliced peppers
1 x 500ml carton passata
1 x 400g tin black beans, drained
1 cup (150g) frozen sweetcorn
3 tsp chipotle paste
1 x 170g tin tinned pink salmon
1 tsp garlic granules
salt and freshly ground black pepper

To cook:
4 tortilla wraps
1 cup (120g) grated Cheddar
  cheese

1   Heat the oil in a large, deep-sided frying pan over a medium heat, then add the onions and garlic and cook, stirring continuously, for 2 minutes, until soft and translucent.

2   Add the sliced peppers, 200ml of the passata, the black beans, sweetcorn and 2 teaspoons of the chipotle paste and stir to combine. Flake in the tinned salmon, removing any pieces of skin or bone as you do, then bring the mixture the boil and cook, stirring occasionally, for 5 minutes. Remove from the heat and set aside to cool.

3   Meanwhile, combine the remaining passata and chipotle paste, reducing the amount of chipotle if you prefer things mild. Add the garlic granules and a generous grinding of salt and pepper and stir to combine.

IF YOU'RE MAKING AHEAD TO *Freeze*...SKIP TO THE BOTTOM

IF YOU'RE COOKING *Now*... Preheat the oven to 180°C/350°F/gas mark 4. Warm the tortilla wraps in the microwave for 15 seconds, then set them on the work surface. Spoon a quarter of the filling mixture into the centre of each wrap, then roll up the sides of tortillas around the filling and place in a large baking dish, seam-side down. Pour the passata and chipotle sauce over the top of the enchiladas, then scatter over the Cheddar cheese. Transfer to the oven for 20 minutes, until golden and bubbling. Serve hot.

IF YOU'RE MAKING AHEAD TO *Freeze*...Once the filling mixture has cooled to room temperature, ladle it into a large, labelled freezer bag, then do the same with the passata sauce, in a separate bag. Freeze both bags flat for up to 3 months. I like to store a packet of wraps beside the sauces in the freezer so that I can grab all 3 out at once.

***Then*...** Remove both sauces and the wraps from the freezer and leave to defrost in the fridge, ideally overnight. Once defrosted, preheat the oven to 180°C/350°F/gas mark 4 and assemble and cook the enchiladas as described above.

THE ULTIMATE CHEESY, CRISPY BACON DIRTY FRIES

Cheesy, bacony, carby heaven – these are SO good! We have a weekly film night with the kids, where we all veg out in front of a movie and enjoy a few indulgent treats after a hard week at work. We rarely agree on the movie but serve up a plate of these and harmony is instantly restored! Pass the remote.

PREP: 10 MINS
COOK: 15–20 MINS
SERVES 4

1 tsp vegetable oil
12 rashers streaky bacon, cut into
  1cm (½ in) slices
50g butter
4 tbsp plain flour
2 cups (480ml) whole milk
2 cups (280g) pre-grated Cheddar
  cheese
2 tsp English mustard
4 spring onions, finely chopped
1 x 200g tin sweetcorn, drained
salt and freshly ground black pepper

To serve:
1 x 900g bag frozen French fries

1 (If you are prepping this to serve straightaway, cook your French fries according to packet instructions now, while you prep the sauce.) Heat the oil in a deep-sided frying pan over a medium heat, then add the sliced bacon and cook, stirring continuously, until crisp and brown. Transfer the bacon to a kitchen paper-lined plate to drain and leave the pan on the heat.

2 Melt the butter in the pan, reducing the heat if it starts to brown, then add the flour and whisk to form a thick paste, cook for 30 seconds, then add the milk a little at a time, whisking and thickening between each addition, until all the milk is used up and you have a glossy sauce.

3 Add the grated Cheddar, mustard, spring onions, sweetcorn, cooked bacon and a generous grinding of salt and pepper, stir until the cheese has melted then remove from the heat.

IF YOU'RE MAKING AHEAD TO *Freeze*...**SKIP TO THE BOTTOM**

IF YOU'RE SERVING *Now*... Transfer the cooked French fries to a serving platter then pour the hot cheesy sauce mixture over the top. Serve hot.

IF YOU'RE MAKING AHEAD TO *Freeze*...
Once the sauce has cooled to room temperature, transfer to a large, labelled freezer bag and freeze flat for up to 3 months. I like to store the sauce alongside the French fries in the freezer.

Then... Remove the sauce from the freezer and leave to defrost fully in the fridge, ideally overnight. Once the sauce is defrosted, cook your French fries according to packet instructions and reheat the sauce in a pan until piping hot. Assemble the dirty fries as described above and serve hot.

BBQ CHICKEN DIRTY FRIES

Dirty fries are a brilliant way of dressing-up a bag of oven chips and turning them into a real treat. These are great for chilling out in front of a movie on a Friday night.

PREP: 10 MINS
COOK: 25–30 MINS
SERVES 4

2 skinless, boneless chicken breasts
1 x 440g bottle barbecue sauce
1 cup (140g) pre-grated mozzarella cheese
1 handful jarred, sliced jalapeno peppers
6 spring onions, finely sliced
1 tbsp white wine vinegar

To serve:
1 x 900g bag frozen French fries
2 tbsp sour cream

1 Preheat the oven to 180°C/350°F/gas mark 4.
2 Wrap the chicken breasts in a foil parcel, place on a baking sheet and transfer to the oven and bake in the oven for 25–30 minutes, until cooked through. (If you are prepping this to serve straightaway, cook your French fries according to packet instructions alongside the chicken.)
3 Meanwhile, combine the barbecue sauce, mozzarella, jalapeno peppers, spring onions and vinegar in a large saucepan and put over a medium heat, stirring occasionally, until bubbling and thickened.
4 Once the chicken is cool enough to handle, use two forks to shred the chicken, then add to the sauce mixture, stir through and remove from the heat.

IF YOU'RE MAKING AHEAD TO *Freeze*...**SKIP TO THE BOTTOM**

IF YOU'RE SERVING *Now*... Transfer the cooked French fries to a serving platter then pour the barbecue sauce and chicken mixture over the top. Dot the sour cream over the surface of the dirty fries, then serve hot.

IF YOU'RE MAKING AHEAD TO *Freeze*...
Once the sauce has cooled to room temperature, transfer to a large, labelled freezer bag and freeze flat for up to 3 months. I like to store the sauce alongside the French fries in the freezer.

Then... Remove the sauce from the freezer and leave to defrost fully in the fridge, ideally overnight. Once the sauce is defrosted, cook your French fries according to packet instructions and reheat the sauce in a pan until piping hot, adding a splash of water to loosen if needed. Assemble the dirty fries as described above and serve hot.

DIRTY PIZZA FRIES

Pizza or chips? Why not have both! If you've got kids in the house, they'll devour this – as will the adults! I pull this out on those times when my house is loaded with hungry teenagers who want something tasty, filling and fun on the table in a hurry.

PREP: 10 MINS
COOK: 15–20 MINS
SERVES 4

1 tsp olive or vegetable oil
2 cups (350g) frozen sliced peppers
1 cup (80g) fresh sliced mushrooms
2 tsp frozen chopped garlic
1 x 500g carton passata
2 tbsp tomato purée
1 tsp dried basil
½ tsp granulated sugar
12 slices pepperoni
1 cup (140g) grated mozzarella

To serve:
1 x 900g bag frozen French fries

1 Heat the oil in a saucepan over a medium heat, then add the peppers, mushrooms and garlic and cook for 3–4 minutes, until softened. Add the passata, tomato purée, basil and sugar and stir to combine. Bring to a boil, then reduce the heat to a simmer and continue to cook, stirring occasionally, for 15 minutes. (If you are prepping this to serve straightaway, cook your French fries according to packet instructions while the sauce is bubbling.)

2 Remove from the heat, stir in the grated mozzarella and pepperoni slices until the cheese is melted and stringy, then set aside.

IF YOU'RE MAKING AHEAD TO *Freeze*...**SKIP TO THE BOTTOM**

IF YOU'RE SERVING *Now*... Transfer the cooked French fries to a serving platter then pour the hot pizza sauce mixture over the top. Serve hot.

IF YOU'RE MAKING AHEAD TO *Freeze*...
Once the sauce has cooled to room temperature, transfer to a large, labelled freezer bag and freeze flat for up to 3 months. I like to store the sauce alongside the French fries in the freezer.

Then... Remove the sauce from the freezer and leave to defrost fully in the fridge, ideally overnight. Once the sauce is defrosted, cook your French fries according to packet instructions and reheat the sauce in a pan until piping hot. Assemble the dirty fries as described above and serve hot.

WELSH RAREBIT DIRTY FRIES

Welsh rarebit is the ultimate comfort food, or it was until this dirty fry recipe was invented!
Crispy chips coated in a velvety blanket of cheese sauce, ripe for dunking and dipping. Heaven!
These also happen to be veggie, so are a great option if you want something indulgent but are trying
to cut down on meat.

PREP: 10 MINS
COOK: 15–20 MINS
SERVES 4

50g butter
4 tbsp plain flour
2 cups (480ml) milk
2 cups (180g) pre-grated Cheddar
  cheese
2 tbsp Worcestershire sauce
2 tsp English mustard
salt and freshly ground black pepper

To serve:
1 x 900g bag oven chips

1 (If you are prepping this to serve straightaway, cook your French fries according to packet instructions now, while you prep the sauce.) Melt the butter in a pan over a low heat, then add the flour and whisk to form a thick paste, cook for 30 seconds, then add the milk a little at a time, whisking and thickening between each addition, until all the milk is used up and you have a glossy sauce.

2 Add the grated Cheddar, Worcestershire sauce, English mustard and a generous grinding of salt and pepper, stir until the cheese has melted then remove from the heat.

IF YOU'RE MAKING AHEAD TO *Freeze*...SKIP TO THE BOTTOM

IF YOU'RE SERVING *Now*... transfer the cooked French fries to a serving platter then pour the hot cheesy sauce mixture over the top. Serve hot.

IF YOU'RE MAKING AHEAD TO *Freeze*...
Once the sauce has cooled to room temperature, transfer to a large, labelled freezer bag and freeze flat for up to 3 months. I like to store the sauce alongside the French fries in the freezer.

***Then*...** Remove the sauce from the freezer and leave to defrost fully in the fridge, ideally overnight. Once the sauce is defrosted, cook your French fries according to packet instructions and reheat the sauce in a pan until piping hot. Assemble the dirty fries as described above and serve hot.

10
Tinned Tuna & Salmon
MEALS IN
1 HOUR

↓

YOU WILL BE MAKING

| SALMON ENCHILADAS | TUNA & SWEETCORN CARBONARA | TUNA MELT PANINIS | SMOKY SWEET POTATO SALMON CAKES | TUNA HASH BAKE |

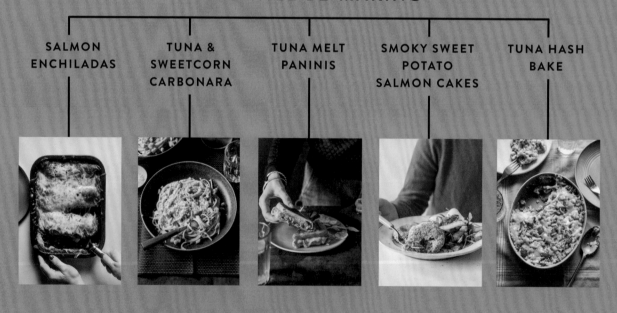

Tinned salmon and tuna are such an economical way of getting fish into your diet and this menu will fill your freezer with 10 delicious fish-based meals, all feeding 4 people. These recipes can be found elsewhere in the book as single recipes but in this section, they are woven together and scaled up into double portions to help you fill your freezer in one dedicated batching session. Read through the recipe first to get a general view of how it is going to work and what equipment you will need to have on hand. The shopping list below includes everything you will need, and I've scaled up the ingredients so you know what pack sizes to buy of each. Lay the ingredients out in piles according to the groupings under the ingredients title overleaf, then follow the numbered guide and you can't go wrong!

Shopping list

Fresh

2 bunches spring onions

2 x 250g bags pre-grated Cheddar cheese

600ml double cream

1 x 100g bag pre-grated Parmesan cheese

2 x 800g packs ready-made mashed potatoes

3 x 450g packs ready-made sweet potato mash

2 x 250g packs cherry tomatoes

2 lemons

8 panini rolls

1 red onion

Frozen

2 x 500g packs frozen chopped onions

1 x 100g pack frozen chopped garlic

1 x 500g pack frozen sliced peppers

1 x 1kg pack frozen sweetcorn

Storecupboard

2 x 200g tins sweetcorn

16 x 145g tins tuna in water

2 x 418g tins pink salmon

1 jar mayonnaise

6 eggs

1 x 150g pack panko breadcrumbs

100g jar chipotle paste

2 x 500g cartons passata

2 x 400g tins black beans

1 jar garlic granules

INGREDIENTS

GET ORGANISED! Before you start make sure that your kitchen surfaces are cleared down, then lay all the ingredients out in individual piles according to the groupings on this page. It is also a good idea to prepare and label your freezer bags.

SALMON ENCHILADAS

2 tbsp olive or vegetable oil
2 cups (230g) frozen chopped onions
4 tsp frozen chopped garlic
2 cups (350g) frozen sliced peppers
2 x 500g cartons passata
2 x 400g tins black beans, drained
2 cups (300g) frozen sweetcorn
6 tsp chipotle paste
1 x 418g tin pink salmon, skin and big bones removed
2 tsp garlic granules

To cook:
8 wraps
2 cups (240g) pre-grated Cheddar cheese

TUNA & SWEETCORN CARBONARA

2 tbsp olive or vegetable oil
2 cups (230g) frozen chopped onions
4 tsp frozen chopped garlic
2½ cups (600ml) double cream
4 x 145g tins tuna, drained
2 x 200g tins sweetcorn, drained
100g pre-grated Parmesan cheese

TUNA HASH BAKE

1 tbsp olive or vegetable oil
4 cups (460g) frozen chopped onions
4 x 145g tins tuna, drained
2 x 800g packs ready-made mashed potatoes
10 spring onions, finely sliced
2 x 250g packs cherry tomatoes, halved
2 lemons, juiced
2 cups (240g) pre-grated Cheddar cheese

TUNA MELT PANINIS

4 x 145g tins tuna, drained
1 red onion, finely diced
4 heaped tbsp mayonnaise
8 handfuls pre-grated Cheddar cheese
8 panini rolls
salt and freshly ground black pepper

SMOKY SWEET POTATO SALMON CAKES

3 x 425g packets pre-made sweet potato mash
1 x 418g tin salmon, skin and big bones removed
4 tsp chipotle paste
4 eggs, beaten
2 cups (90g) panko breadcrumbs
salt and freshly ground black pepper

METHOD

SALMON ENCHILADAS

1 Heat the oil in a large, deep-sided frying pan over a medium heat, then add the onions and garlic and cook, stirring continuously, for 2 minutes, until soft and translucent.

2 Add the sliced peppers, 1 carton of the passata, the black beans, sweetcorn and 4 teaspoons of the chipotle paste and stir to combine. Flake in the tinned salmon, removing any pieces of skin or bone as you do, then bring the mixture the boil and cook,

stirring occasionally, for 5 minutes. Remove from the heat and set aside to cool.

3 Combine the remaining carton of passata and 2 teaspoons of chipotle paste in a bowl, reducing the amount of chipotle if you prefer things mild. Add the garlic granules and a generous grinding of salt and pepper and stir to combine. Divide the mixture between 2 labelled freezer bags and set aside.

TUNA & SWEETCORN CARBONARA

4 Heat the oil in a large, deep-sided frying pan, then add the onions and garlic and cook for 2–3 minutes, until soft.

5 Add the double cream, tuna, sweetcorn, Parmesan and a generous grinding of salt and pepper, then

stir to combine and cook for 2–3 minutes, until bubbling and slightly thickened. Remove from the heat and set aside to cool to room temperature.

TUNA HASH BAKE

6 Heat the oil in a large, deep-sided frying pan over a medium heat, then add the onions and garlic and cook, stirring continuously, for 2–3 minutes, until soft.

7 Tip the cooked onions and garlic into a large mixing bowl, then add the tuna, spring onions, tomatoes and lemon juice and crumble in the mashed potatoes.

8 Give everything a mix to combine, then divide the mixture between 2 medium baking dishes, pressing

the surface of each down into an even layer. Scatter over the grated Cheddar.

9 Cover the unbaked hash with a lid or wrap in a layer of clingfilm followed by a layer of foil, label and freeze flat for up to 3 months. (If you don't have 2 baking dishes or freezer space is at a minimum, freeze the mixture in 2 large, labelled freezer bags and omit the grated cheese until you come to cook the Tuna Hash Bake later.

TUNA MELT PANINIS

10 Flake the tuna into a bowl, then stir through the red onion, mayonnaise and a grinding of salt and pepper.

11 Slice open the panini rolls and spread 1 half of each roll with the tuna and onion mixture.

12 Top the tuna-spread half of each panini roll with a handful (around ½ cup/90g) of pre-grated Cheddar cheese, then sandwich the rolls with the untopped halves of the rolls.

13 Wrap each of the uncooked paninis in foil, then transfer to a large, labelled freezer bag and freeze flat for up to 3 months.

SMOKY SWEET POTATO SALMON CAKES

14 Crumble the sweet potato mash into a large bowl, then add the salmon, chipotle paste and a generous grinding of salt and pepper. Mix well to bring everything together.

15 Turn the mixture out onto a clean work surface and divide it into 2 halves. Using your hands, divide each half into 8 equal portions, then form each portion into a ball. Once you have formed 16 balls, use your hands to press them down into thick patties.

16 Set two shallow bowls on the work surface. Crack the eggs into the first bowl and beat lightly to combine. Put the panko breadcrumbs in the second bowl.

17 Working with one at a time, dip the fishcakes first in the beaten egg, then in the breadcrumbs to coat completely. Set aside on a plate or a sheet of baking paper while you coat the remaining fishcakes.

18 Divide the fishcakes between 2 foil-lined baking sheets and put both sheets in the freezer to flash freeze for 1 hour, then transfer the fishcakes to 2 large, labelled freezer bags and freeze for up to 3 months.

SALMON ENCHILADAS CONTINUED...

19 Once the filling mixture has cooled to room temperature, divide it between 2 large, labelled freezer bags. Freeze the bags of enchilada filling and the separate bags of passata sauce flat for up to 3 months

TUNA & SWEETCORN CARBONARA CONTINUED...

20 Once the Carbonara sauce has cooled to room temperature, divide it between 2 large, labelled freezer bags and freeze flat for up to 3 months.

Congratulations
You now have 10 family meals for four ready for the freezer!

WHEN YOU COME TO COOK

SALMON ENCHILADAS

Remove a bag of enchilada filling and a bag of spiced passata sauce from the freezer and leave to defrost in the fridge, ideally overnight. Once defrosted, preheat the oven to 180°C/350°F/gas mark 4. Warm the tortilla wraps in the microwave for 15 seconds, then set them on the work surface. Spoon a quarter of the filling mixture into the centre of each wrap, then roll up the sides of tortillas around the filling and place in a large baking dish, seam-side down. Pour the passata and chipotle sauce over the top of the enchiladas, then scatter over the Cheddar cheese. Transfer to the oven for 20 minutes, until golden and bubbling. Serve hot.

TUNA & SWEETCORN CARBONARA

Remove the sauce from the freezer and leave to defrost in the fridge, ideally overnight. Once defrosted, tip the sauce into a pan and reheat over a low heat slowly so that the sauce doesn't split, adding a splash of water if necessary, until piping hot all the way through. While the sauce is cooking, boil dried spaghetti until tender, then serve the sauce over bowls of cooked pasta.

TUNA MELT PANINIS

Remove individual paninis from the freezer as needed. Unwrap the foil, then place in the microwave on defrost for 2 minutes. Once defrosted, toast in a preheated panini maker for 4 minutes, until crisp and the cheese is melted and bubbling.

TUNA HASH BAKE

This can be cooked directly from frozen. Preheat the oven to 180°C/350°F/gas mark 4, cover the baking dish with foil (removing any clingfilm if you used it to wrap the dish before freezing) and transfer to the oven for 40 minutes, then remove the foil and cook for another 20 minutes, until golden.

SMOKY SWEET POTATO SALMON CAKES

These can be cooked straight from frozen. Lay the frozen fishcakes on a foil-lined baking sheet and transfer to an oven preheated to 180°C/350°F/gas mark 4 and bake for 40 minutes, until crisp, golden and piping hot all of the way through.

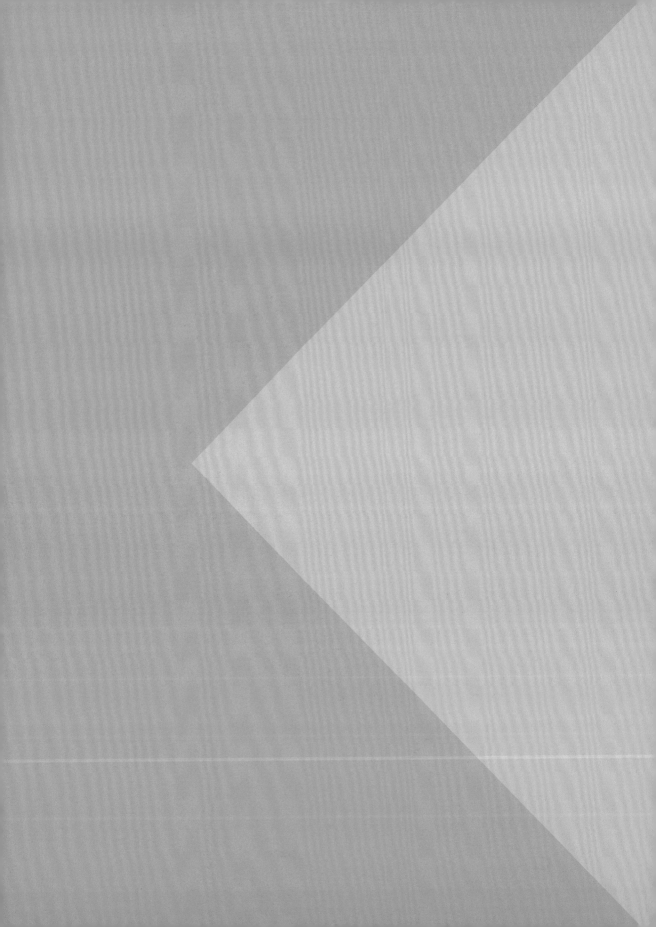

EASY ENTERTAINING

BEETROOT & FETA FILO PIE

This delicious open pie can be served hot or cold and is delicious served with a light salad for lunch or bulked out with new potatoes and greens for a substantial dinner. The earthy beetroot and tangy feta complement each other wonderfully.

PREP: 10 MINS
COOK: 25–30 MINS
SERVES 4

500g cooked beetroot
1 x 390g tin cooked green lentils, drained
1 tsp dried thyme
200g feta cheese
6 sheets filo pastry
olive oil, for brushing
salt and freshly ground black pepper

1 Preheat the oven to 180°C/350°F/gas mark 4 and brush a medium-sized ovenproof dish with olive oil.
2 Pat the beetroot dry with kitchen paper to remove any moisture, then chop into small cubes and add to a large mixing bowl along with the drained lentils and dried thyme. Crumble in two-thirds of the feta cheese, then give the mixture a thorough stir and set aside.
3 Layer 2 sheets of the filo pastry in the oiled ovenproof dish so that the pastry comes up the sides and any excess overhangs. Brush the top sheet of pastry generously with olive oil, then add another two sheets of pastry. Repeat until all 6 sheets of pastry are used up and the top layer is brushed with oil.
4 Tip the filling into the pie and spread out evenly, then crumble over the remaining feta cheese.

IF YOU'RE MAKING AHEAD TO *Freeze*...SKIP TO THE BOTTOM

IF YOU'RE COOKING TO SERVE *Now*... Transfer the pie to the preheated oven and leave to cook for 25–30 minutes, until the pastry is crisp and golden and the filling is piping hot. Cut into wedges and serve hot or cold.

IF YOU'RE MAKING AHEAD TO *Freeze*... bake the pie as above, but remove from the oven after 20 minutes and set aside to cool to room temperature. Once cooled, wrap the pie and its dish in a layer of foil followed by a layer of clingfilm, then label and freeze flat for up to 3 months.

***Then*...** The pie can either be cooked straight from frozen or defrosted overnight in the fridge before reheating. If defrosting first, remove the foil and clingfilm and reheat the pie in an oven heated to 180°C/350°F/gas mark 4 until piping hot all the way through. If cooking direct from frozen, increase the cooking time to 35–40 minutes and cover the pie with a layer of foil to prevent the pastry from catching.

ROAST BUTTERNUT SQUASH WITH A COUSCOUS CRUST

Roasting butternut squash in this way brings out its natural sweetness and delicious earthy flavours. Bulked up with fluffy couscous this is substantial enough to make a main meal, but would also work as a side dish or even a dinner party starter.

PREP: 10 MINS
COOK: 70 MINS
SERVES 4

glug of olive or vegetable oil
1 large butternut squash, topped, tailed, cut into quarters and seeds removed
½ cup (100g) couscous
½ cup (120ml) boiling water
100g feta cheese
juice of 1 lemon
2 heaped tbsp pesto
8 cherry tomatoes, cut into quarters
salt and freshly ground black pepper
olive oil, for roasting

1 Preheat the oven to 180°C/350°F/gas mark 4. Add a glug of oil to a lipped baking sheet and place in the oven to warm.
2 Once the oil is hot, add the butternut wedges to the tray, turning to coat in the hot oil as you do. Bake for 40 minutes, turning halfway through, until the squash is golden and just tender.
3 While the squash is cooking, transfer the couscous to a large bowl and pour over ½ cup (120ml) of boiling water. Cover and set aside for 5 minutes, then fluff the couscous up with a fork.
4 Crumble the feta into the bowl, then add the lemon juice, pesto, cherry tomatoes and a generous grinding of salt and pepper. Stir to combine.

IF YOU'RE MAKING AHEAD TO *Freeze*...**SKIP TO THE BOTTOM**

IF YOU'RE COOKING *Now*... Spoon the couscous mixture over the roasted squash slices and return to the oven for another 30 minutes. Divide the squash wedges between serving plates and serve.

Zhuzh it up...
With a good drizzle of balsamic glaze

IF YOU'RE MAKING AHEAD TO *Freeze*...
Set the squash and couscous aside until cooled to room temperature, then transfer the squash wedges to a large freezer bag and the couscous to a smaller bag. Seal the couscous bag and then place inside the bag with the squash before sealing. Label and freeze flat for up to 3 months.

Then... Remove the squash and couscous from the freezer and place in the fridge to defrost, ideally overnight. Once defrosted lay the squash on a foil-lined baking sheet and spoon over the couscous. Transfer to an oven preheated to 180°C/350°F/gas mark 4 and bake for 30 minutes, until piping hot all the way through. Serve as above.

AUBERGINE & PEANUT CURRY

This makes a great meat-free option for evenings when you want to put something full of flavour on the table with minimum fuss. It makes a great Friday night option for easy entertaining when you might have otherwise reached for the takeaway menu.

PREP: 5 MINS
COOK: 15 MINS
SERVES 4

1 tbsp vegetable oil
1 cup (115g) frozen chopped onions
1 tsp frozen chopped garlic
1 tsp frozen chopped ginger
2 tbsp mild curry powder
2 large aubergines, cut into bite-sized pieces
1 cup (175g) frozen mixed peppers
2 tbsp tomato purée
2 x 400g cans coconut milk
¼ cup (50g) peanut butter (crunchy or smooth is fine)
1 tbsp lemon juice
cooked basmati rice and naan breads, to serve

1 Heat the oil in a large saucepan over a medium heat, then add the onions, garlic and ginger and cook, stirring, until the onions are soft and translucent.

2 Add the curry powder, diced aubergines, peppers and tomato purée to the pan and stir to combine. Continue to cook for 2 minutes, stirring occasionally.

3 Add the coconut milk, peanut butter and lemon juice to the pan and stir to combine. Bring to simmer, then reduce the heat to low and leave to cook for around 10 minutes, until the aubergine is tender and the sauce has thickened.

IF YOU'RE MAKING AHEAD TO *Freeze*...**SKIP TO THE BOTTOM**

IF YOU'RE SERVING *Now*... Simply spoon the curry into serving bowls and serve with cooked basmati rice and naan breads alongside.

IF YOU'RE MAKING AHEAD TO *Freeze*...
Set the curry aside to cool to room temperature, then ladle into a large, labelled freezer bags and freeze flat for up to 3 months.

Then... Remove the bag from the freezer and leave to defrost in the fridge, ideally overnight. Once defrosted, tip the curry into a large pan and warm over a medium heat until piping hot all of the way through. Serve as above.

CHICKEN & MUSHROOM HUMBLE PIE

This is the kind of pie that cold days are made for. Easy to prep and a cinch to assemble from frozen if you get organised and make the filling ahead, I like to keep a batch of this in the freezer ready for comfort food emergencies.

PREP: 10 MINS
COOK: 35–40 MINS
SERVES 6

1 tbsp olive or vegetable oil
1 cup (115g) frozen chopped onions
4 skinless, boneless chicken thighs,
 cut into bite-sized pieces
300g chestnut mushrooms, sliced
2 tbsp plain flour
1 cup (240ml) chicken stock
scant 1 cup (200ml) milk
1 tsp wholegrain mustard
1 sheet pre-rolled puff pastry
1 egg, beaten
salt and freshly ground black pepper

MAKE IT
Veggie!
Replace the chicken with quorn pieces for a delicious vegetarian alternative.

1 Heat the oil in a large, deep-sided frying pan over a medium heat, then add the onions and chicken pieces and cook, stirring, until the onions are soft and the chicken is sealed. Add the sliced mushrooms to the pan and stir to combine with the chicken and onions, then cook, stirring occasionally, for 5–7 minutes until the chicken is cooked through and the mushrooms have released all their water.

2 Add the flour to the pan and stir to coat the chicken and vegetables, then pour in the chicken stock and stir well. Slowly pour in the milk, stirring and thickening the sauce as you do, then bring the mixture to the boil, reduce the heat to low and leave to cook for 10–15 minutes, until thickened, then stir through the mustard and season well with salt and pepper. Remove from the heat and set aside.

IF YOU'RE MAKING AHEAD TO *Freeze*...**SKIP TO THE BOTTOM**

IF YOU'RE COOKING *Now*... Preheat the oven to 180°C/350°F/gas mark 4. Pour the pie filling into a large, ovenproof baking dish smaller than the sheet of pastry, then lay the pastry over the top of the filling and tuck in the edges. Brush the top of the pie with the beaten egg, then transfer the pie to the oven for 30–35 minutes, until golden and well risen. Cut into generous wedges and serve hot with mash and veg alongside, if you like.

IF YOU'RE MAKING AHEAD TO *Freeze*...Leave the filling mixture to cool to room temperature, then ladle into a large, labelled freezer bag and freeze flat with the sheet of pastry alongside for up to 3 months.

Then... Remove the pie filling and pastry sheet from the freezer and leave to defrost in the fridge, ideally overnight. Once defrosted, preheat the oven to 180°C/350°F/gas mark 4 and assemble, cook and serve the pie in the same way described above.

FETA & SQUASH RISOTTO

Risotto has long been a favourite in my house – the whole family love it! This is homely and comforting, but also feels luxurious enough for a dinner party or special family dinner. Just don't tell anyone how easy it is to make!

PREP: 10 MINS
COOK: 25–30 MINS
SERVES 4

500g frozen butternut squash
  chunks
2 tbsp olive oil
2 tsp dried thyme
1 cup (115g) frozen diced onions
2 tsp frozen chopped garlic
285g (2 cups) risotto rice
5 cups (1.2 litres) vegetable stock
  (use 2 stock cubes)
2 heaped tbsp grated Parmesan
100g feta cheese, crumbled
salt and freshly ground black pepper

1 Preheat the oven to 180°C/350°F/gas mark 4 and line a large baking sheet with foil.
2 Lay the frozen butternut squash pieces on the baking sheet, scatter with the thyme and drizzle over 1 tablespoon of the olive oil. Give everything a mix to ensure the squash is well coated, then spread out in an even layer and transfer to the oven for 25 minutes, until tender.
3 Meanwhile, heat the remaining olive oil in a large, ovenproof saucepan with a lid over a medium heat. Add the onions and garlic and cook for 2–3 minutes, stirring, until soft and translucent.
4 Add the rice to the pan and stir to coat in the oil and onions, then continue to cook, stirring, for about a minute to gently toast the grains. Pour in the vegetable stock and give everything a stir, then bring the mixture to the boil and cover the pan with a lid.
5 Transfer the pan to the oven and bake the risotto for 18 minutes. Once cooked, remove the pan from the oven and give the risotto a stir. There may still be some liquid, but the risotto should thicken as you stir it. Add the cooked butternut squash pieces, Parmesan, feta and a generous grinding of salt and pepper and stir again.

IF YOU'RE MAKING AHEAD TO *Freeze*...**SKIP TO THE BOTTOM**

IF YOU'RE COOKING *Now*... Simply spoon the hot risotto into serving bowls and enjoy.

IF YOU'RE MAKING AHEAD TO *Freeze*...
Set the pan aside until the risotto has cooled to room temperature, then spoon into large, labelled freezer bags and freeze flat for up to 3 months.

Then... Remove the risotto from the freezer and leave to defrost in the fridge, ideally overnight. Once fully thawed, reheat the risotto in a saucepan over a medium heat or in a bowl in the microwave until piping hot. If the risotto mixture is too dry, stir in a bit of water to loosen it up while heating.

SPANISH CHICKEN TRAYBAKE

This couldn't be easier to prep ahead and have in your freezer ready to pull out for a midweek meal or any low-key emergency entertaining. I like to double-up and stock my freezer with a couple of these type of no-cook, dump-bag meals as part of my weekly batching as they really are the work of moments.

PREP: 5 MINS
COOK: 45 MINS
SERVES 4

8 new potatoes, halved
8 chicken drumsticks
2 red onions, roughly chopped
2 tsp frozen chopped garlic
2 tsp smoked paprika
2 tsp dried oregano
1 red pepper, deseeded and sliced
1 yellow pepper, deseeded and
　sliced
1 courgette, cut into bite-sized
　pieces
salt and freshly ground black pepper
olive oil, for drizzling

1　Put the new potatoes in a small pan and cover with cold water. Place over a high heat and bring to the boil, then reduce the heat to a simmer and cook for 5 minutes, until parboiled. Drain.

IF YOU'RE MAKING AHEAD TO *Freeze*...SKIP TO THE BOTTOM

IF YOU'RE COOKING *Now*... Preheat the oven to 180°C/350°F/gas mark. Put the parboiled potatoes along with all the other ingredients in a large ovenproof baking dish, season generously with salt and pepper and give everything a good mix to combine. Drizzle with a little olive oil, then transfer to the oven to cook for 45 minutes, until is cooked and golden. Spoon onto serving plates and serve hot.

Zhuzh it up...

By adding some diced chorizo and sprinkling over some fresh chopped parsley.

IF YOU'RE MAKING AHEAD TO *Freeze*...Once the potatoes have cooled to room temperature, transfer all of the ingredients to a large, labelled freezer bag and freeze flat for up to 3 months.

***Then*...** Remove the bag from the freezer and leave to defrost fully in the fridge, ideally overnight. Once defrosted, preheat the oven to 180°C/350°F/gas mark 4 and cook the traybake as described above.

PENNY SAVING PAELLA

Who would have thought paella could be budget friendly? By using a bag of frozen seafood mix you cut down on so much cost and extra waste. This is a great entertaining recipe that will transport you to Spain and won't cost the earth. **NOTE:** Once defrosted and cooked, this recipe cannot be reheated.

PREP: 10 MINS
COOK: 20 MINS
SERVES 4

2 tbsp olive oil
1 cup (115g) frozen chopped onions
2 tsp frozen chopped garlic
80g frozen diced chorizo
1 tsp smoked paprika
300g paella rice
1 x 400g can chopped tomatoes
500ml fish stock (1 stock cube)
2 tsp frozen chopped parsley

To serve:
1 x 400g pack frozen mixed
   seafood, defrosted on the day you
   want to serve your paella
1 lemon, cut into quarters

1   Heat the oil in a large, deep-sided frying pan over a medium heat. Add the onions, garlic, chorizo and cook, stirring, until the onions are soft and the chorizo has released its oils and is fragrant.

2   Add the smoked paprika and paella rice to the pan and stir until everything is well coated in the spice and chorizo oil, then add the chopped tomatoes and fish stock to the pan and stir again. Bring to the boil, then reduce the heat to a simmer and leave to cook for 10 minutes, stirring occasionally.

IF YOU'RE MAKING AHEAD TO *Freeze*...**SKIP TO THE BOTTOM**

IF YOU'RE COOKING *Now*... Continue to cook the rice, stirring occasionally, for another 8 minutes. Meanwhile, heat a splash of olive oil in another frying pan over a medium heat, then add your defrosted seafood mix and cook, stirring, for 3–4 minutes, until all of the fish and seafood is cooked through. Tip the cooked seafood into the paella and stir to combine. Spoon into serving dishes and serve immediately with wedges of lemon alongside.

IF YOU'RE MAKING AHEAD TO *Freeze*...
Remove the rice from the heat and set aside to cool to room temperature (it's ok that your rice is slightly undercooked at this point). Once cooled, spoon the mixture into a large, labelled freezer bag and freeze flat for up to 3 months. I like to put the rice and frozen seafood mixture next to each other in the freezer so I can grab them both out to defrost at the same time.

Then... Remove the rice and seafood mixture from the freezer and leave both to fully defrost in the fridge, ideally overnight. Once fully defrosted, tip the rice mixture into a large, microwavable bowl and reheat in the microwave for 6–8 minutes, stirring occasionally, until piping hot all of the way through. Meanwhile, heat a splash of olive oil in a frying pan over a medium heat, then add your defrosted seafood mix and cook, stirring, for 3–4 minutes, until all of the fish and seafood is cooked through. Tip the cooked seafood into the reheated paella rice and stir to combine. Serve hot, with lemon wedges alongside.

10
Butternut Squash & Sweet Potato
MEALS IN
1 HOUR

↓

YOU WILL BE MAKING

| ROAST BUTTERNUT SQUASH WITH A COUSCOUS CRUST | FETA & SQUASH RISOTTO | SWEET POTATO & CHICKPEA ONE POT | SWEET POTATO MISO MEDLEY | SQUASH, BEETROOT & GOAT'S CHEESE PUFF ROLL |

This is perhaps my favourite of the 10 Meals in 1 Hours sections in this book. The recipes are easy, delicious and a great way of adding an extra hit of veg to your diet. These recipes can be found elsewhere in the book but in this section they are woven together and scaled up into double portions to help you fill your freezer. Read through the recipe first to get a general view of how it is going to work and what equipment you will need. The shopping list below includes everything you will need, and I've scaled up the ingredients so you know what pack sizes to buy of each. Lay the ingredients out in piles according to the groupings under the ingredients heading overleaf, then follow the numbered guide and you can't go wrong!

Shopping list

Fresh

2 large butternut squash

2 x 200g packs feta cheese

1 x 330g pack cherry tomatoes

1 x 100g pack pre-grated Parmesan cheese

2 x 150g logs goat's cheese

2 sheets pre-rolled puff pastry

1 x 500g pack cooked beetroot

Frozen

4 x 500g packs frozen butternut squash chunks

4 x 500g packs frozen sweet potato chunks

2 x 500g packs frozen chopped onions

1 x 100g pack frozen chopped garlic

1 x 100g pack frozen chopped parsley

1 x 500g pack frozen sliced peppers

Storecupboard

1 x 500g pack dried couscous

1 jar pesto

1 small bottle olive or vegetable oil

1 jar dried thyme

1 x 500g pack risotto rice

6 vegetable stock cubes

2 x 400g tins chickpeas

4 x 400g tins chopped tomatoes

1 jar smoked paprika

1 jar dried oregano

2 x 400g cans butter beans

100g jar white miso paste

2 x 400g tins coconut milk

1 bottle lemon juice

INGREDIENTS PER RECIPE

GET ORGANISED! Before you start make sure that your kitchen surfaces are cleared down, then lay all the ingredients out in individual piles according to the groupings on this page. It is also a good idea to prepare and label your freezer bags.

ROAST BUTTERNUT SQUASH WITH A COUSCOUS CRUST

2 large butternut squash, top, tailed, cut into
quarters and seeds removed
1 cup (200g) couscous
1 cup (240ml) boiling water
200g feta cheese, crumbled
6 tbsp lemon juice
4 heaped tbsp pesto
16 cherry tomatoes, quartered

FETA & SQUASH RISOTTO

2 x 500g packs frozen butternut squash chunks
4 tbsp olive or vegetable oil
4 tsp dried thyme
2 cups (230g) frozen chopped onions
4 tsp frozen chopped garlic
2½ cups (500g) risotto rice
7½ cups (1.8 litres) vegetable stock
4 heaped tbsp pre-grated Parmesan cheese
200g feta cheese, crumbled
salt and freshly ground black pepper

SQUASH, BEETROOT & GOATS CHEESE PUFF ROLL

2 x 500g bags frozen butternut squash chunks
4 tbsp olive or vegetable oil
4 tsp dried thyme

1 x 500g pack cooked beetroot
2 x 150g packs goat's cheese cut into chunks
2 sheets ready-rolled puff pastry
4 tbsp pesto

To serve
1 egg, beaten

SWEET POTATO & CHICKPEA ONE POT

2 cups (230g) frozen chopped onions
4 tsp frozen chopped garlic
2 x 500g bags frozen sweet potato chunks
2 x 400g tins chickpeas, drained
4 x 400g tins chopped tomatoes
4 tsp smoked paprika
2 tsp dried oregano
2 tbsp frozen chopped parley
2 vegetable stock cubes

SWEET POTATO MISO MEDLEY

2 cups (230g) frozen chopped onions
4 tsp frozen chopped garlic
2 x 500g bags frozen sweet potato chunks
2 cups (350g) frozen sliced peppers
1 jar white miso paste
2 x 400g tins butter beans, drained
2 x 400g tins coconut milk

METHOD

ROAST BUTTERNUT SQUASH WITH A COUSCOUS CRUST

1 Preheat the oven to 180°C/350°F/gas mark 4. Add a glug of olive oil to a lipped baking sheet and place in the oven to warm.

2 Add your 8 butternut wedges to the tray, turning to coat in the oil as you do. Bake for 40 minutes, turning halfway through, until the squash is just tender.

FETA & SQUASH RISOTTO & SQUASH, BEETROOT & GOAT'S CHEESE PUFF ROLL

3 Divide the frozen butternut squash pieces for both recipes between 2 large baking sheets, scatter with the thyme and drizzle 2 tablespoons of oil over each tray. Transfer to the oven (at the same temperature as the squash wedges, above) for 25 minutes, until tender.

FETA & SQUASH RISOTTO CONTINUED...

4 Heat the remaining 2 tablespoons of olive oil in a lidded ovenproof saucepan over a medium heat. Add the onions and garlic and cook for 2–3 minutes, stirring, until soft and translucent.

5 Add the rice to the pan and stir to coat in the oil, then cook, stirring, for about a minute. Pour in the vegetable stock and give everything a stir, then bring to the boil, reduce to a simmer and cook, stirring every 3–4 minutes, for 18 minutes, until the rice is tender and has absorbed the stock.

ROAST SQUASH WITH A COUSCOUS CRUST CONTINUED...

6 Transfer the couscous to a bowl and pour over 1 cup (240ml) of boiling water. Stir, then cover and set aside.

SWEET POTATO & CHICKPEA ONE POT

7 Divide all of the ingredients between 2 large, labelled freezer bags and freeze flat for up to 3 months.

SWEET POTATO MISO MEDLEY

8 Divide all of the ingredients between 2 large freezer bags and freeze flat for up to 3 months.

FETA & SQUASH RISOTTO CONTINUED...

9 Remove both trays of butternut squash from the oven. Add one of the trays of squash to the risotto along with the Parmesan and feta cheese. Stir well and season to taste. Set aside to cool.

ROAST SQUASH WITH A COUSCOUS CRUST CONTINUED...

10 Fluff the couscous up with a fork, then crumble the feta into the bowl, add the lemon juice, pesto, cherry tomatoes and a generous grind of salt and pepper. Stir to combine.

11 Divide the couscous mixture between 2 labelled freezer bags and set aside.

SQUASH, BEETROOT & GOATS CHEESE PUFF ROLL CONTINUED...

12 Drain the beetroot and cut each ball into 8 slices. Put the beetroot slices in a large bowl along with the crumbled goats' cheese and the remaining cooled butternut squash chunks. Mix well to combine.

13 Unroll both sheets of puff pastry, keeping them on their baking paper lining, and set them in front of you so that the wider edges are at the top and bottom. Using a sharp knife, lightly score a horizontal line through the middle of each sheet of pastry to divide them into 2 equal halves, being sure not to cut all the way through the pastry.

14 Leaving a 2.5cm (1in) border around the edge of the pastry, divide the squash and beetroot mixture between the top halves of the pastry sheets and form each into an even rectangular shape with your hands.

15 Leaving a 2.5cm (1in) border around the edge, evenly spread the pesto over the bottom half of each sheet.

16 Brush the borders you have left around each sheet of pastry with the beaten egg, then bring the bottom halves of the pastry up and over the top halves to encase the filling. Use a fork to press all around the edges of the pastry to seal.

17 Wrap the uncooked puff rolls up tightly in their baking paper wrappers, then wrap again in a couple of layers of clingfilm. Label each roll clearly and freeze for up to 3 months.

ROAST SQUASH WITH A COUSCOUS CRUST CONTINUED...

18 Remove the squash wedges from the oven and set aside to cool to room temperature.

FETA & SQUASH RISOTTO CONTINUED...

19 Once your risotto has cooled to room temperature, divide it between 2 large, labelled freezer bags and freeze flat for up to 3 months.

ROAST SQUASH WITH A COUSCOUS CRUST CONTINUED...

20 Once the wedges of butternut squash have cooled, divide them between to 2 large, labelled freezer bags, adding a smaller bag of couscous to each bag before sealing. Freeze flat for up to 3 months.

WHEN YOU COME TO COOK

ROAST BUTTERNUT SQUASH WITH A COUSCOUS CRUST

Remove the squash and couscous from the freezer and place in the fridge to defrost, ideally overnight. Once defrosted lay the squash on a foil-lined baking sheet and spoon over the couscous. Transfer to an oven preheated to 180°C/350°F/gas mark 4 and bake for 30 minutes, until piping hot all the way through. Serve hot.

SQUASH, BEETROOT & GOAT'S CHEESE PUFF ROLL

This can be cooked from frozen or defrosted first. To cook from frozen, simply unwrap the puff roll, place on a baking paper-lined baking sheet and brush the top and sides with a little egg wash. Transfer to an oven preheated to 180°C/350°F/gas mark 4 and leave to bake for 1 hour, until golden, covering with foil if it starts to catch. To cook from defrosted, put the puff roll in the fridge overnight and allow to defrost, then cook in the same way, but reducing the cooking time to 40 minutes.

SWEET POTATO & CHICKPEA ONE POT

Remove the bag from the freezer and leave to defrost fully in the fridge, ideally overnight. Once defrosted, tip all the ingredients and 1 cup (240ml) boiling water into a large pan over a medium heat and bring to the boil, stirring occasionally. Reduce the heat to a simmer, then leave to cook for 15–20 minutes, stirring occasionally, until everything is tender. Ladle into bowls and serve hot.

SWEET POTATO MISO MEDLEY

Remove the bag from the freezer and leave to fully defrost in the fridge, ideally overnight. Once defrosted, tip the medley into a large pan over a medium heat and stir to combine. Bring to the boil, then reduce the heat to a simmer and leave to cook, stirring occasionally, for 15–20 minutes, until the vegetables are tender. Spoon into serving bowls and serve hot.

FETA & SQUASH RISOTTO

Remove the risotto from the freezer and leave to defrost in the fridge, ideally overnight. Once fully thawed, reheat the risotto in a saucepan over a medium heat or in a bowl in the microwave until piping hot. If the risotto mixture is too dry, stir in a bit of water to loosen it up while heating.

COFFEE SHOP CLASSICS

CINNAMON SWIRLS

These coffee-house favourites are so easy to make at home and can be kept in your freezer and baked off when friends pop over unannounced. They make a great treat breakfast and kids will love to get involved with the icing.

PREP: 8 MINS
COOK: 20–25 MINS
MAKES: 10

70g soft butter
2 tbsp brown sugar
1 tsp ground cinnamon
1 sheet pre-rolled puff pastry

For the icing:
4 tbsp icing sugar
1–2 tsp water

1 Put the butter, sugar and cinnamon in a small bowl and beat well to combine.
2 Unroll the sheet of puff pastry, keeping it on its baking paper lining, and set it on the work surface in front of you so that the shorter edges are at the top and bottom.
3 Leaving a 1cm (½in) border all around the edge of the pastry, spread the spiced butter mixture over the pastry in an even layer.
4 Working from one of the shorter ends and using the backing paper to help, roll the pastry into a tight cylinder. Once rolled, cut the pastry in half, then cut each half into 5 equal discs, so that you end up with 10 swirls.

IF YOU'RE MAKING AHEAD TO *Freeze*...SKIP TO THE BOTTOM

IF YOU'RE COOKING *Now...* Spread the swirls out over 2 lined baking sheets, spacing them out to allow them spread during cooking. Transfer to an oven preheated to 200°C/400°F/gas mark 6 and leave to cook for 15–18 minutes, until puffed, golden and crisp. Set aside to cool for 10 minutes. Meanwhile, make the icing by beating the icing sugar with enough of the water to make a thick, smooth, drizzleable paste. Drizzle the icing over the swirls and serve warm.

IF YOU'RE MAKING AHEAD TO *Freeze*...
Lay the unbaked swirls on a lined baking tray and transfer to the freezer to flash-freeze for 1 hour. Once frozen, transfer the swirls to a large, labelled freezer bag and freeze flat for up to 3 months.

Then... These are best cooked straight from frozen. spread the swirls out over 2 lined baking sheets, spacing them out to allow them spread during cooking. Transfer to an oven preheated to 200°C/400°F/gas mark 6 and leave to cook for 20–25 minutes, until puffed, golden and crisp. Set aside to cool for 10 minutes. Make the icing and serve the swirls as described above.

BANANA & RAISIN OATY BARS

Oats are a fantastic way to stop the tummy rumbles as they are slow energy releasing, so these make the perfect grab-and-go breakfast snack. Grab one of these from the freezer on your way out of the door and it will be defrosted and ready to eat by the time you get to your desk!

PREP: 8–10 MINS
COOK: 25 MINS
MAKES: 10 BIG BARS

4 ripe bananas
1 tsp ground cinnamon
2 tbsp butter
4 tbsp peanut butter
3 tbsp golden syrup
3½ cups (400g) porridge oats
2 large handful raisins

1 Preheat the oven to 180°C/350°F/gas mark 4. Grease a 23 x 23cm (9 x 9 inch) square cake tin and line with baking paper.
2 Peel the bananas and add them to a large mixing bowl with the cinnamon. Using a fork, mash the bananas until smooth, then set aside.
3 Put the butter, peanut butter and golden syrup in a small pan over a low heat and warm gently until everything has melted together.
4 Pour the melted butter mixture into the bowl with the bananas, then add the porridge oats and raisins and give everything a good stir until thoroughly combined.
5 Tip the mixture into the prepared cake tin and press down in an even layer with the back of a wooden spoon. Transfer to the preheated oven and bake for 25 minutes, until golden.
6 Set aside to cool to room temperature, then remove from the tin and cut into 12 equal slices.

IF YOU'RE MAKING AHEAD TO *Freeze*...SKIP TO THE BOTTOM

IF YOU'RE SERVING *Now*... These are now ready to be served. They make a brilliant breakfast or mid-afternoon boost when your energy is running low.

IF YOU'RE MAKING AHEAD TO *Freeze*...Simply, lay the slices in a large, labelled freezer bag in a single layer, then freeze flat for up to 3 months.

Then... Remove individual bars from the freezer as needed and defrost at room temperature for an hour before eating.

BRAN LOAF

This is an old family recipe that has been part of my baking repertoire since I was a teenager. The ingredients need time to soak, so I tend to prep them the evening before I want to bake and leave them overnight. I promise it's more than worth the wait, and doing it this way means you can bake the loaf in the morning and have a slice generously slathered in butter for an indulgent breakfast

PREP: 10 MINS, PLUS OVERNIGHT SOAKING
COOK: 1HR 25 MINS
MAKES: 8 SLICES

1 cup (190g) caster sugar
1 cup (150g) dried fruit
1 cup (60g) bran flakes
1 cup (240ml) milk
1 cup (160g) self-raising flour
½ tsp baking powder

1 Put the sugar, dried fruit, bran flakes and milk in a large bowl, then cover and put in the fridge to soak for at least an hour or up to overnight.

2 When you are ready to bake, preheat the oven to 180°C/350°F/gas mark 4 and grease and line a 450g (1lb) loaf tin with baking paper.

3 Add the flour and baking powder to the bowl with the soaked ingredients and stir until all the ingredients are well combined. Tip the mixture into the prepared loaf tin and level out the surface with a spatula.

4 Transfer to middle of the oven to bake for 1 hour 20 minutes, until an inserted skewer comes out clean. If the loaf needs a bit more cooking, return to the oven for another 5 minutes, then test again.

5 Leave the cooked loaf to cool in its tin for 10 minutes, then turn out and set aside to cool to room temperature.

IF YOU'RE MAKING AHEAD TO *Freeze*...**SKIP TO THE BOTTOM**

IF YOU'RE SERVING *Now*... Cut the loaf into thick slices and serve slathered with salty butter. This is best eaten the day after baking, but can be wrapped in clingfilm and stored for up to 4 days if needed.

IF YOU'RE MAKING AHEAD TO *Freeze*...Cut the loaf in half (each half gives you 4 slices) and wrap each half in a layer of foil followed by a layer of clingfilm. Label clearly and freeze for up to 3 months.

Then... Remove the loaf halves from the freezer as needed and leave to defrost at room temperature for 2 hours before slicing and serving. The defrosted loaf will keep for up to 4 days.

CARROT SHEET CAKE

Sheet cake is a brilliant alternative to a layered cake as it can be portioned easily and can be frozen once baked, then simply iced after defrosting. This is a really economical (and delicious!) recipe that is perfect for feeding a crowd.

PREP: 5 MINS
COOK: 30–35 MINS
MAKES: 12 GENEROUS SLICES

2 cups (420g) caster sugar
1 cup (240ml) vegetable oil
4 eggs
2 cups (270g) grated carrots
2 cups (220g) plain flour
2 tsp baking powder
1 tsp bicarbonate of soda
2 tsp ground cinnamon
1 tsp mixed spice

For the icing:
150g butter, at room temperature
400g cream cheese
1 cup (145g) icing sugar
1 tsp vanilla extract

1 Preheat the oven to 180°C/350°F/gas mark 4 and grease a 23 x 33cm (9 x 13 inch) rectangular cake tin and line with baking paper.

2 In a large mixing bowl, combine the sugar, oil, eggs, carrots, flour, baking powder, bicarbonate of soda, cinnamon and mixed spice and beat together with an electric whisk until well combined.

3 Pour the mixture into the tin and level out with a spatula, then transfer to the preheated oven to bake for 30–35 minutes, until an inserted skewer comes out clean. Set the cake aside to cool for 10 minutes in the tin, then carefully remove from the tin and leave to cool to room temperature.

4 While the cake is cooling, make the icing by beating the butter in a large mixing bowl for 2 minutes with an electric whisk, until light and fluffy. Add the cream cheese and continue to beat on a low speed until well incorporated. Sift in the icing sugar and add the vanilla extract, then beat on a low speed again until smooth, creamy and well combined.

IF YOU'RE MAKING AHEAD TO *Freeze*...SKIP TO THE BOTTOM

IF YOU'RE SERVING *Now*... Spread the icing over the cooled cake with a spatula or palette knife, ensuring the cake is covered right to the edges. You can make a decorative pattern through the icing with a fork, if you like. Slice the cake into 12 equal squares and enjoy – perfect with a nice cup of tea alongside!

IF YOU'RE MAKING AHEAD TO *Freeze*...Once the cake has fully cooled, wrap the whole thing in a layer of foil followed by a layer of clingfilm, then label clearly and freeze flat for up to 3 months. If your freezer is very full, you can return the wrapped cake to the tin and freeze them both together to help the cake retain its shape. Put the icing is a small, labelled freezer bag and freeze alongside the cake.

Then... Remove the cake and icing from the the freezer and defrost fully in the fridge, ideally overnight. Once defrosted the icing may look a bit lumpy, but that can be easily fixed by tipping into a mixing bowl and beating with an electric whisk until it comes together. Ice, slice and serve the cake as described above.

VEGAN CHOCOLATE CUPCAKES

These delicious chocolate cupcakes just happen to be vegan, so are perfect for whipping out when your plant-based friends come over for tea and cake! I like to serve these slightly warm from the microwave for an extra indulgent treat.

PREP: 10 MINS
COOK: 25 MINS
MAKES: 12

1¾ cups (220g) plain flour
½ cup (40g) cocoa powder
1 cup (200g) caster sugar
1 tsp bicarbonate of soda-
½ tsp baking powder
½ tsp salt
1 cup (240ml) plant-based milk
  (oat, almond or soya work well)
⅓ cup (80ml) vegetable oil
1 tsp vanilla extract
1 tbsp white wine vinegar
1 cup (175g) vegan chocolate chips,
  plus a few extra for finishing

1   Preheat the oven to 180°C/350°F/gas mark 4 and line a 12-hole muffin tin with cases – I like to use tulip style cases for that coffee shop look.
2   In a large mixing bowl, combine the flour, cocoa powder, sugar, bicarbonate of soda, baking powder and salt.
3   In a separate jug, combine the plant-based milk, vegetable oil, vanilla extract and white wine vinegar, then pour the wet ingredients into the dry ingredients and mix well to a smooth batter. Add 1 cup (175g) of the chocolate chips and fold through the mixture. Spoon the muffin mixture into the prepared cases, then scatter over the reserved chocolate chips.
4   Transfer to the oven to bake for 25 minutes, until an inserted skewer comes out clean. Set aside to cool to room temperature.

IF YOU'RE MAKING AHEAD TO *Freeze*...**SKIP TO THE BOTTOM**

IF YOU'RE SERVING *Now*... The muffins are now ready to eat. I like mine still slightly warm from the oven with a scoop of vanilla ice cream alongside.

IF YOU'RE MAKING AHEAD TO *Freeze*...
Once the muffins have cooled completely, transfer to a large, labelled freezer bag in a single layer and freeze flat for up to 3 months.

Then... Remove the muffins from the freezer and set aside at room temperature to defrost. This will take 30–60 minutes. If you'd like to serve them slightly warm, microwave the muffins for a few seconds before serving.

CARAMEL CRUNCH SPECULOOS TRAYBAKE

Speculoos are a deep caramel flavoured biscuit which goes so well with white chocolate. I like to freeze these in individual slices to grab from the freezer whenever I hear the call of the coffee shop. They defrost is about an hour, so are the perfect standby for when you have friends coming over for coffee.

PREP: 10 MINS, PLUS
2–3 HOURS SETTING
MAKES: 12 SLICES

100g butter
1 x 390g can condensed milk
600g speculoos biscuits
200g white chocolate, broken into
  pieces

1 Line a 20 x 30cm (8 x 12 inch) rectangular cake tin with baking paper.
2 Put the butter and condensed milk in a large pan over a low heat and warm until the butter has completely melted, then remove from the heat.
3 Meanwhile, put the biscuits in large freezer bag and whack with a rolling pin until crushed. I like to leave a few large pieces of biscuit in with my crumbs to add a bit of texture. Alternatively, this can be done in a food processor.
4 Add the crushed biscuits to the pan with the butter and condensed milk and stir until everything is well combined. Tip the mixture into the prepared cake tin and use the back of a wooden spoon to press down in an even layer that fills right to the corners of the tin. Transfer to the fridge to set for 1 hour.
5 When the speculoos mixture is almost set, bring a small pan of boiling water to a simmer over a low heat. Place a heatproof bowl over the pan, ensuring the base does not touch the water, then add the white chocolate to the bowl and stir until fully melted. (You can also melt the chocolate in the microwave in 20 second increments on low power, if you prefer.)
6 Pour the melted chocolate over the speculoos base and use a palette knife to spread in an even layer. Put the traybake in the fridge until fully set, this will take 2–3 hours.
7 Once set, remove the traybake from the tin by pulling up on the edge of the baking paper. Cut into 12 equal-sized pieces (or more if you prefer).

IF YOU'RE MAKING AHEAD TO *Freeze*...SKIP TO THE BOTTOM

IF YOU'RE SERVING *Now*... The slices are now ready to serve. Enjoy with a warm cup of tea or coffee.

IF YOU'RE MAKING AHEAD TO *Freeze*...Lay the slices in a large freezer bag or airtight container and transfer to the freezer for up to 3 months.

***Then*...** Remove individual slices from the freezer and set aside to defrost at room temperature as needed. The slices should defrost in about an hour.

CHOCOLATE CRUNCH TRAYBAKE

This tastes incredible, takes no time at all and contains just 5 ingredients, making it the ultimate easy teatime treat! This is a great one to get the kids involved with, so why not stock the freezer with a few yummy snacks and have some fun along the way!

PREP: 10 MINS, PLUS
3 HOURS SETTING
MAKES: 12 SLICES

100g butter
1 x 397g can condensed milk
400g milk chocolate digestives
200g milk chocolate, broken into
  pieces
3 tbsp cocoa powder

1 Line a 20 x 30cm (8 x 12 inch) rectangular cake tin with baking paper.
2 Put the butter and condensed milk in a large pan over a low heat and warm until the butter has completely melted, then remove from the heat.
3 Meanwhile, put the biscuits in large freezer bag and whack with a rolling pin until crushed. I like to leave a few large pieces of biscuit in with my crumbs to add a bit of texture. Alternatively, this can be done in a food processor.
4 Add the crushed biscuits to the pan with the butter and condensed milk and stir until everything is well combined. Tip the mixture into the prepared cake tin and use the back of a wooden spoon to press down in an even layer that fills right to the corners of the tin. Transfer to the fridge to set for 1 hour.
5 When the digestive mixture is almost set, bring a small pan of boiling water to a simmer over a low heat. Place a heatproof bowl over the pan, ensuring the base does not touch the water, then add the chocolate to the bowl and stir until fully melted. (You can also melt the chocolate in the microwave in 20 second increments on low power, if you prefer.)
6 Pour the melted chocolate over the digestive base and use a palette knife to spread in an even layer. Put the traybake in the fridge until fully set, this will take 2–3 hours.
7 Once set, remove the traybake from tin by pulling up on the edge of the baking paper. Cut into 12 equal-sized pieces (or more if you prefer).

IF YOU'RE MAKING AHEAD TO *Freeze*...SKIP TO THE BOTTOM

IF YOU'RE SERVING *Now*... The slices are now ready to serve. These make great tea-time snacks or are perfect with a mid-morning coffee.

IF YOU'RE MAKING AHEAD TO *Freeze*...
Lay the slices in a large freezer bag or airtight container and transfer to the freezer for up to 3 months.

Then... Remove individual slices from the freezer and set aside to defrost at room temperature as needed. The slices should defrost in about an hour. These make great additions to a picnic, as they can be packed in the morning and will be defrosted by lunch.

WONKY FRUIT TARTS

These little tarts make a lovely fruity treat for your child's lunchbox. They can be served cold as a quick pick-me-up or dressed up with ice cream and served warm for a child-friendly dessert.

PREP: 10 MINS
COOK: 12–14 MINS
MAKES 12 TARTS

1 sheet pre-rolled shortcrust pastry
1 x 340g jar raspberry jam
200g frozen berries
icing sugar, to dust

1   Preheat the oven to 180°C/350°F/gas mark 4 and grease a 12-hole muffin tin.

2   Unroll the sheet of shortcrust pastry on a lightly floured surface and use a 10cm (4 inch) round cutter to stamp out as many circles as possible. Clump any remaining pastry together and use a rolling pin to roll out again, until all of the pastry is used up.

3   Push 1 round of pastry down into each hole in the prepared muffin tin so that the sides come up and form a rough tart case. These look lovely if they're a bit wonky, so don't worry if they're not perfectly uniform.

4   Spoon a heaped tablespoon of raspberry jam into each mini tart case and top with a few frozen berries, then transfer the tin to the preheated oven for 12–14 minutes, until the pastry is crisp and golden.

5   Remove the tarts from the oven and leave to cool slightly in the tin, then use a palette knife to carefully remove from the tarts from the tin.

IF YOU'RE MAKING AHEAD TO *Freeze*...SKIP TO THE BOTTOM

IF YOU'RE SERVING *Now*... They can be served warm or cooled to room temperature. Simply dust with a little icing sugar, transfer to serving plates and enjoy!

IF YOU'RE MAKING AHEAD TO *Freeze*...
Leave the tarts to cool to room temperature, then add them to a large, labelled freezer bag in a single layer. Freeze flat for up to 3 months.

Then... Remove as many tarts as you need from the freezer and set aside to defrost at room temperature, this will take about an hour. Enjoy cold, or warm for 30 seconds or so in the microwave before serving.

DESSERTS

APPLE & CINNAMON CRUMBLE

This warm hug of a pudding is an absolute classic and is the perfect way to finish off a Sunday lunch with friends and family. Make it ahead and cook straight from the freezer and you've got a homemade dessert that can be on the table in a flash.

PREP: 10 MINS
COOK: 30–35 MINS
SERVES 6

3 medium cooking apples, peeled, cored and finely sliced
2 tsp ground cinnamon
3 tbsp caster sugar

For the crumble topping:
2 cups (220g) plain flour
140g butter, cut into cubes
½ cup (100g) brown sugar
1 tsp ground cinnamon

1 Put the apple slices, cinnamon and caster sugar in a large saucepan over a medium heat. Add a splash of boiling water, then bring the apples to a simmer and leave to cook, stirring occasionally, for about 5 minutes, until the apples have softened. Pour the apples into a medium baking dish and set aside.

2 To make the crumble, put the flour and butter in a large mixing bowl then rub the butter into the flour with your fingers to create a golden rubble that resembles breadcrumbs. Add the sugar and cinnamon to the bowl and stir to combine.

3 Spread the crumble mixture over the top of the apples in an even layer that reaches right to the edges of the dish.

IF YOU'RE MAKING AHEAD TO *Freeze*...**SKIP TO THE BOTTOM**

IF YOU'RE COOKING *Now*... Preheat the oven to 180°C/350°F/gas mark 4. Once the oven is hot, cook the crumble for 30–35 minutes, covering with tin foil if the top starts to catch, until golden and bubbling. Scoop into serving bowls and serve hot, with lashings of custard, cream or ice cream alongside.

IF YOU'RE MAKING AHEAD TO *Freeze*... Leave the unbaked crumble aside until the filling has cooled to room temperature. Once cooled, cover the dish with a lid (if your dish has one) or wrap in a layer of foil followed by a layer of clingfilm, then label and freeze flat for up to 3 months.

Then... This can be baked directly from frozen. Simply preheat the oven to 180°C/350°F/gas mark 4, unwrap the crumble and bake for 40–50 minutes, covering with tin foil if the top starts to catch, until golden and bubbling.

BAKED, SPICED COCONUT RICE PUDDINGS

This is wonderfully fragrant take on a traditional rice pudding, rich with juicy currants and a mellow note of coconut. It makes a wonderful finish to an Indian meal, when you want something sweet to finish but want to carry a fragrant note of spice through the courses. This makes 4 individual puddings for which you'll need 4 small ramekins.

PREP: 5 MINS
COOK: 1 HOUR 15 MINS
SERVES 4

4 tsp butter
½ cup (100g) pudding rice
4 tbsp raisins
4 tbsp caster sugar
1 tsp ground cinnamon
1 tsp mixed spice
1 x 400ml tin coconut milk
1¾ cups (420ml) whole milk
double cream, to serve (optional)

1   Preheat the oven to 150°C/300°F/gas mark 2 and grease 4 small ramekins with a teaspoon of butter each.
2   Put 25g of pudding rice, 1 tablespoon of raisins and 1 tablespoon of caster sugar in each ramekin. Set the ramekins on a baking sheet.
3   Combine the cinnamon, mixed spice, coconut milk and whole milk in a large jug and stir to combine. Divide the milk mixture between the 4 ramekins, then give each ramekin a gentle stir to ensure the rice is well distributed in the milk mixture.
4   Transfer the baking sheet to the oven and leave the puddings to cook for 45 minutes.

IF YOU'RE MAKING AHEAD TO *Freeze*...**SKIP TO THE BOTTOM**

IF YOU'RE SERVING *Now*... Remove the rice puddings from the oven and give them a gentle stir, then return to the oven for an additional 30 minutes, until the rice is plump and tender. I like to stir a splash of double cream into each ramekin just before serving to make the puddings extra indulgent.

IF YOU'RE MAKING AHEAD TO *Freeze*... Remove the rice puddings from the oven and give them a gentle stir, then return to the oven for an additional 20 minutes, at which point the rice will still be slightly firm. Stir again and set aside to cool to room temperature, then wrap the ramekins in a layer of foil followed by a layer of clingfilm and freeze flat for up to 3 months.

Then... Remove the puddings from the freezer and leave to defrost fully in the fridge, ideally overnight. Once the rice puddings are fully defrosted, preheat the oven to 150°C/300°F/gas mark 2 and set the ramekins on a baking sheet. Bake the puddings for 10–15 minutes, until piping hot all the way through and serve as described above.

PEACH & RASPBERRY COBBLER

This classic American dish is a wonderfully comforting dessert. It's made with fruit from the freezer and storecupboard, so providing the cupboards aren't bare it's a really easy dish to whip up when you don't have any fresh fruit in, or when it's out of season. Feel free to experiment with the fruit and use up anything that you have to hand.

PREP: 10 MINS
COOK: 40 MINS
SERVES 6

butter, for greasing
2 x 400g tins peaches in juice, drained
1 cup (70g) frozen raspberries
2 tbsp caster sugar
1 tsp ground ginger
double cream, to serve (optional)

For the cobbler topping:
1 cup (120g) self-raising flour
100g butter, cut into cubes
¼ cup (50g) caster sugar

1   Preheat the oven to 180°C/350°F/gas mark 4 and grease a medium baking dish with butter.
2   Put the drained peaches and frozen raspberries in the base of the baking dish, ensuring that they are evenly distributed, then sprinkle over the caster sugar and ground ginger. Set aside while you make the topping.
3   Put the flour, butter and caster sugar in the bowl of a food processor and pulse together until you have a mixture that resembles breadcrumbs. (If you don't have a food processor, add the ingredients to a large mixing bowl and rub the butter into the flour and sugar until you have a rubbly, breadcrumb consistency.) Add 4 tablespoons of water to the mixture and use your hands to bring together to a soft dough.
4   Arrange large spoonfuls of the dough over the surface of the cobbler – don't worry if you have gaps, the cobbler will spread as it cooks. Transfer to the oven for 40 minutes, until the topping is golden and the filling is soft and bubbling.

IF YOU'RE MAKING AHEAD TO *Freeze*...**SKIP TO THE BOTTOM**

IF YOU'RE SERVING *Now*... Leave the cobbler to cool slightly for 5 minutes, then spoon into serving bowls and serve warm with a drizzle of cream, if you like.

IF YOU'RE MAKING AHEAD TO *Freeze*... Set the cobbler aside until cooled to room temperature. Once cooled, cover the dish with a lid (if your dish has one) or wrap in a layer of foil followed by a layer of clingfilm, then label and freeze flat for up to 3 months.

Then... Remove the cobbler from the freezer and defrost in the fridge, ideally overnight. Once defrosted, preheat the oven to 180°C/350°F/gas mark 4, unwrap the cobbler and reheat for 20–25 minutes, until golden and bubbling. Serve as above.

JAM ROLY-POLY

PREP: 10 MINS
COOK: 45 MINS
SERVES 6

butter, for greasing
2 cups (220g) self-raising flour
100g shredded suet
2 tbsp caster sugar
zest of 1 lemon
½ cup plus 2 tbsp (150ml) semi-skimmed milk
1 tsp vanilla extract
5–6 tbsp raspberry jam
ice cream or custard, to serve
(optional)

1 Preheat the oven to 180°C/350°F/gas mark 4. Half fill a roasting tin with boiling water and place on the base of the oven, then position an oven shelf as close as possible to the top of the roasting tin.

2 Cut a 35cm (14 inch) length of foil and the same length of baking paper. Set the foil flat on the worktop and lay the baking paper over the top, then grease the surface of the paper all over with butter. Set aside.

3 Combine the flour, suet, caster sugar and lemon zest in a large bowl and make a well in the centre. Pour the milk and vanilla extract into the well, then use your hands to bring together to a rough dough. Turn the dough onto a lightly floured surface and knead for 5 minutes, until smooth.

4 Using a rolling pin, roll the dough out to a 30 x 20cm (12 x 8 inch) rectangle, then spread the jam over the surface, leaving a 2cm (¾ inch) border around the outside edge.

5 Starting from one of the narrower ends, roll the dough into a tight spiral, then place the roly-poly in the centre of your sheet of buttered baking paper, in the same orientation as the paper and with the seam in the dough facing down. Bring up the longer sides of your sheets of baking paper and foil and crimp together at the top to form a seal – you don't want it to be too tight. Twists of the ends of the baking paper and foil together to seal like a Christmas cracker.

6 Place the jam roly-poly in the oven, directly on the rack above the roasting tin full of water. Leave to cook for 45 minutes, until well risen. Set aside to cool slightly, then unwrap the pudding being careful of any escaping steam as you do (if you are planning to freeze the roly-poly keep hold of the foil and baking paper as they can be used to package the pudding for the freezer).

IF YOU'RE MAKING AHEAD TO *Freeze*...**SKIP TO THE BOTTOM**

IF YOU'RE SERVING *Now...* Simply cut the roly-poly into thick slices and transfer to serving bowls. Serve hot, with ice cream or custard alongside.

IF YOU'RE MAKING AHEAD TO *Freeze...*
Set the roly-poly aside to cool to room temperature, then rewrap the pudding tightly in its baking paper and foil layers, label and freeze flat for up to 3 months.

Then... Remove from the freezer and leave to defrost in the fridge, ideally overnight. Once defrosted, the pudding can be wrapped loosely in foil and reheated in an oven preheated to 180°C/350°F/gas mark 4 for 20–25 minutes, until piping hot all of the way through, or reheated in the microwave (without any foil!) for 2–3 minutes.

CHOCCY PEAR BAKE

Tinned fruit is such a great thing to have in your cupboard. It's cheap, keeps for ages and is the perfect option to fall back on when you want something sweet and fruity but your fruit bowl is empty. Here, tinned pears are baked into an indulgent chocolate sponge, making for a warming autumnal dessert that the whole family will love.

PREP: 10 MINS
COOK: 40–45 MINS
SERVES 6

150g soft butter, plus extra for greasing
¾ cup (150g) caster sugar
3 eggs, beaten
1¼ cups (140g) self-raising flour
1 tsp baking powder
1 tsp vanilla extract
2 tbsp cocoa powder
splash of milk
1 x 400g tin tinned pears, drained
double cream or custard, to serve (optional)

1 Preheat the oven to 180°C/350°F/gas mark 4 and grease a medium baking dish with butter.
2 Put the butter, caster sugar, eggs, flour, baking powder, vanilla extract, cocoa powder and a splash of milk in a large mixing bowl and beat with an electric whisk to a smooth batter.
3 Tip the drained pears into the base of the prepared baking dish in an even layer, then pour over the batter, spreading out the surface with a spatula.
4 Transfer to the oven to bake for 40–45 minutes, until well risen and an inserted skewer comes out clean. If the pudding needs a little more cooking, return it to the oven for another 5 minutes then check again.

IF YOU'RE MAKING AHEAD TO *Freeze*...**SKIP TO THE BOTTOM**

IF YOU'RE SERVING *Now*... Spoon the pudding into serving bowls and serve hot, doused in lashing of cream or custard.

IF YOU'RE MAKING AHEAD TO *Freeze*...
Set the pudding aside until cooled to room temperature, then cover with a lid or wrap the entire dish in a layer of foil followed by a layer of clingfilm, label and freeze flat for up to 3 months.

Then... Remove from the freezer and leave to defrost in the fridge, ideally overnight. Once defrosted, the pudding can be wrapped loosely in foil and reheated in an oven preheated to 180°C/350°F/gas mark 4 for 20 minutes, until piping hot all of the way through, or reheated in the microwave (without any foil!) for 2–3 minutes.

CHOCOLATE BREAD & BUTTER PUDDING

This deliciously gooey bread and butter pudding, spiked with luxurious chocolate chips, takes a family favourite and elevates it to the next level. Make this whenever you have a loaf of bread that's past its best that needs using up for a thrifty treat that minimises on waste.

PREP: 10 MINS
COOK: 30 MINS
SERVES 6

9 slices of white bread, crusts removed
50g soft butter
100g dark chocolate chips
3 large eggs
1¼ cups (300ml) milk
¾ cup (180ml) double cream, plus extra to serve
1 tsp vanilla extract
2 tbsp cocoa powder
3 tbsp demerara sugar

1 Preheat the oven to 180°C/350°F/gas mark 4.
2 Spread the slices of bread with the butter, then cut in half diagonally so that you have 18 buttered triangles coated in butter. Arrange half of the bread, buttered-side down and slightly overlapping, in a medium baking dish to form an even layer that covers the surface of the dish.
3 Scatter half the chocolate chips over the bread layer, then top with the remaining bread slices.
4 Whisk together the eggs, milk, cream, vanilla extract and cocoa powder in a measuring jug until combined, then pour over the bread mixture in the baking dish. Sprinkle the sugar over the surface of the pudding and scatter over the remaining chocolate chips, then carefully transfer to the oven to bake for 30 minutes, until the surface is crisp and golden and the egg, milk and cream mixture has set.

IF YOU'RE MAKING AHEAD TO *Freeze*...SKIP TO THE BOTTOM

IF YOU'RE SERVING *Now*... Cut the pudding into wedges and serve hot, with double cream alongside for pouring.

IF YOU'RE MAKING AHEAD TO *Freeze*...
Set the bread and butter pudding aside until cooled to room temperature, then cover with a lid or wrap in a layer of clingfilm followed by a layer of foil, label and freeze flat for up to 3 months.

***Then*...** Remove the bread and butter pudding from the freezer and transfer to the fridge to fully defrost, ideally overnight. Once defrosted, preheat the oven to 180°C/350°F/gas mark 4, cover the baking dish with foil (removing any clingfilm if you used it to wrap the dish before freezing) and transfer to the oven for 20 minutes, until piping hot all the way through. Serve as described above.

CHURROS

I like to make a huge vat of these deliciously decadent strips of fried dough and freeze them before cooking so that I can simply grab a few from the freezer every time my family fancies a sweet dessert. Don't worry if you don't have a piping bag, simply cut the corner from a freezer bag and use that instead.

PREP: 10 MINS
COOK: 5–10 MINS
MAKES 30

1 cup (240ml) water
½ cup (110g) salted butter, cubed
1 tsp vanilla extract
pinch of salt
2 tsp ground cinnamon
1 cup (110g) plain flour
3 large eggs
4 cups (960ml) vegetable oil, for deep frying
½ cup (100g) sugar, to serve
chocolate dipping sauce, to serve

1 Put the water, butter, vanilla extract, salt and 1 teaspoon of cinnamon in a large pan over a medium heat and cook until the butter has melted and all the ingredients have come together. Remove the pan from the heat then add the flour and beat together to form a wet batter. Crack in the eggs, one at a time, beating with a wooden spoon to incorporate between each addition, until you have a smooth, glossy dough.

2 Fit a piping bag with a large, star-shaped nozzle if you have one (otherwise just use a large freezer bag with the corner snipped off) and transfer the dough to the bag.

IF YOU'RE MAKING AHEAD TO *Freeze*...SKIP TO THE BOTTOM

IF YOU'RE COOKING *Now*... Put the oil in a large pan or deep-fat fryer and heat to 180°C/350°F, or until a small portion of the batter floats to the surface and fries to a rich golden brown in 2 minutes. Hold the piping pag over the hot oil (low down, so that it doesn't splash) and squeeze out a 7.5cm (3 inch) length of dough, carefully using a pair of scissors to nip it off at the end so that it drops into the oil. Cook in batches of 6 or 7 for 2 minutes on each side, then transfer to a kitchen paper-lined plate while you cook the remainder. Once all the churros are cooked, put the sugar and remaining teaspoon of cinnamon in a large bowl and mix to combine, add the churros to the bowl and toss to coat in the sugar mixture. Serve immediately with melted chocolate alongside for dipping.

IF YOU'RE MAKING AHEAD TO *Freeze*...Line a large baking sheet with baking paper, then pipe 7.5cm (3 inch) lengths of the dough onto the baking sheet, positioning the churros close together, until all of the dough is used up. Transfer the baking sheet to the freezer to flash-freeze the churros for 1 hour, until firm, then transfer to a large, labelled freezer bag and freeze for up to 3 months.

***Then*...** Remove as many frozen churros from the freezer as you need. Put the oil in a large pan or deep-fat fryer and heat to 180°C/350°F, or until a small portion of the batter floats to the surface and fries to a rich golden brown in 2 minutes. Cook the churros in batches of 6 or 7 for 2 minutes on each side, then toss in the sugar and cinnamon and serve as described above.

OREO PEANUT BUTTER ICE CREAM CAKE

This looks so impressive and makes a wonderful dessert for a celebration or even a great substitute to a birthday cake but is really only an assembly job that takes minimal effort to prep. If your family aren't fans of peanut butter, try chocolate hazelnut spread instead.

PREP: 10 MINS, PLUS 3 HOURS SETTING
SERVES 6

1 x 154g packet Oreos
60g butter, melted, plus extra for greasing
200g chocolate digestive biscuits
80g smooth peanut butter, plus a little extra to drizzle over the top
1 x 900ml tub of vanilla ice cream, softened

1   Grease an 18cm (7 inch) springform tin with butter and set aside.
2   Set aside 3 Oreos to use for decoration, then add the rest to a large freezer bag along with the digestive biscuits and smash with a rolling pin to fine crumb consistency. Transfer to a large mixing bowl, add the melted butter and stir to combine. Tip the crumb mixture into the prepared springform tin and press down into the base in an even layer. Transfer to the fridge to firm up while you prepare the topping.
3   Tip the ice cream into a mixing bowl (it should be soft but not runny). Put the peanut butter in a separate small microwavable bowl and microwave for a few seconds until runny, then pour the peanut butter into the ice cream and beat together with a wooden spoon until combined.
4   Remove the base from the fridge and pour over the ice cream mixture, levelling it out in an even layer. Dot a little more peanut butter over the surface, then use a knife or skewer to ripple through the ice cream.
5   Crush the remaining oreos and sprinkle over the top, then cover the ice cream cake with clingfilm and transfer to the freezer for at least 3 hours to set.

IF YOU'RE MAKING AHEAD TO *Freeze*...**SKIP TO THE BOTTOM**

IF YOU'RE SERVING *Now*... Once the ice cream cake has fully set, remove from the freezer and leave to thaw slightly for around 10 minutes. Run a knife around the inside edge of the tin, then open the springform tin, cut the cake into wedges and serve.

IF YOU'RE MAKING AHEAD TO *Freeze*...
Simply leave the cake in the freezer for up to 3 months.

Then... Remove the cake from the freezer and leave to thaw slightly for around 10 minutes. Run a knife around the inside edge of the tin, then open the springform tin, cut the cake into wedges and serve.

STICKY TOFFEE APPLE PUDDING

Substituting traditional dates for apples in this sticky toffee pudding recipe is a great way of keeping the cost down while still getting everyone's favourite dessert on the table!

PREP: 10 MINS
COOK: 35 MINS
SERVES 6

For the sponge:
100g butter, plus extra for greasing
¾ cup (150g) light brown sugar
2 eggs
1¾ cup (200g) self-raising flour
1 tsp baking powder
1 tsp bicarbonate of soda
1 pinch salt
3 tbsp black treacle
1 tsp vanilla extract
½ cup (120ml) whole milk
1 medium sized cooking apple, peeled and diced into small chunks
double cream or ice cream, to serve

For the sauce:
75g butter
¼ cup (50g) light brown sugar
1 cup (240ml) double cream
½ teaspoon vanilla essence
1 tbsp black treacle
pinch of salt

1 Preheat the oven to 180°C/350°F/gas mark 4 and grease a medium baking dish with butter.
2 Put the butter, sugar, eggs, flour, baking powder, bicarbonate of soda, salt, treacle and vanilla extract in a large bowl and beat with an electric whisk until well combined. Add the milk a little at a time, whisking to incorporate between each addition, until it is all used up.
3 Add the apple to the bowl and fold through the batter, then pour the mixture into your prepared baking dish and transfer to the oven to cook for 35 minutes, until an inserted skewer comes out clean.
4 While the sponge is baking, make the sauce by putting all of the ingredients in a pan over a medium heat, stirring until everything has melted together into a smooth sauce. Cook for 1 minute more, then remove from the heat and set aside.
5 Once the sponge is cooked through, stab the top all over with a skewer, then pour the sauce all over the top so that it soaks down through the holes you have just made.

IF YOU'RE MAKING AHEAD TO *Freeze*...SKIP TO THE BOTTOM

IF YOU'RE SERVING *Now*... Scoop the pudding into bowls and serve hot with lashings of double cream or ice cream alongside.

IF YOU'RE MAKING AHEAD TO *Freeze*...
Set the pudding aside until cooled to room temperature, then cover with a lid or wrap in a layer of clingfilm followed by a layer of foil, label and freeze flat for up to 3 months.

Then... Remove the pudding from the freezer and transfer to the fridge to fully defrost, ideally overnight. Once defrosted, preheat the oven to 180°C/350°F/gas mark 4, cover the baking dish with foil (removing any clingfilm if you used it to wrap the dish before freezing) and transfer to the oven for 20–25 minutes, until piping hot all the way through. Serve as described above.

ONE JOINT, FOUR WAYS

Roast Chicken
4 WAYS

↓

YOU WILL BE MAKING

| ROAST CHICKEN | CHICKEN, PEPPER & CHICKPEA CURRY | CAJUN CHICKEN PASTA BAKE | CHICKEN, PESTO & MOZZARELLA QUESADILLA WRAPS |

Cooking a whole roast chicken and using all of the meat is much more economical than buying expensive breast meat. If you wanted to go an extra step you could even boil the chicken carcasses after stripping off the meat to make a tasty stock that's better than anything you'll ever get from a cube! This menu shows you how to take 2 roast chickens and turn them into 4 delicious family meals for the freezer.

Shopping list

Fresh

2 large chickens

250g cherry tomatoes

2 x 240g mozzarella balls

500g natural yoghurt

Frozen

1 x 500g pack frozen chopped onions

1 pack frozen chopped garlic

1 x 500g pack frozen sliced peppers

1 pack frozen chopped ginger

Storecupboard

1 small bottle olive or vegetable oil

1 pack tortilla wraps

1 x 190g jar pesto

2 x 400g tins chopped tomatoes

2 x 500g cartons passata

1 pack chicken stock cubes

1 jar Cajun spice mix

1 x 500g pack dried pasta (penne or fusilli work well)

1 jar curry powder

1 jar ground cumin

1 x 400g tin chickpeas

INGREDIENTS

ROAST CHICKEN

2 large chickens

olive or vegetable oil, for drizzling

salt and freshly ground black pepper

CHICKEN, PEPPER & CHICKPEA CURRY

1 tbsp olive or vegetable oil

1 cup (115g) frozen chopped onions

2 tsp frozen chopped garlic

1 tsp frozen chopped ginger

1 tbsp curry powder

1 tsp ground cumin

1 x 400g tin chopped tomatoes

1 x 500g carton passata

½ cup (120ml) chicken stock

1 cup (175g) frozen sliced peppers

1 x 400g tin chickpeas, drained

2 heaped tbsp natural yoghurt

half the roast chicken pieces
(see step 12 of method)

CAJUN CHICKEN PASTA BAKE

1 tbsp olive or vegetable oil

1 cup (115g) frozen chopped onions

1 tsp frozen chopped garlic

1 x 400g tin chopped tomatoes

1 x 500g carton passata

½ cup (120ml) chicken stock

1 cup (175g) frozen sliced peppers

2–3 tsp Cajun spice mix

350g dried pasta
(penne or fusilli work well)

1 x 240g ball mozzarella cheese,
drained and shredded

half the roast chicken pieces
(see step 12 of method)

CHICKEN, PESTO & MOZZARELLA QUESADILLA WRAPS

8 slices roast chicken
(see step 12 of method)

4 tortilla wraps

4 tbsp pesto

8–10 cherry tomatoes, roughly chopped

1 x 240g ball mozzarella, drained
and shredded

METHOD

ROAST CHICKEN

1 Preheat the oven to 180°C/350°F/gas mark 4.
2 Put the chickens in a large roasting tin (or divide between 2 if you don't have one large enough), season with salt and pepper and drizzle with a little oil.
3 Transfer to the oven to roast for 1 hour 30 minutes, until golden, juicy and cooked all of the way through. (Chickens vary in size, so do check the cooking times on the packaging and adjust accordingly.)
4 Clean down the kitchen sides, then go and do something else until the chickens have 30 minutes left in the oven.

CHICKEN, PEPPER & CHICKPEA CURRY

5 Heat the oil in a large pan over a medium heat, then add the onions, garlic and ginger and cook for 2–3 minutes, stirring continuously, until soft.
6 Add the curry powder, cumin, chopped tomatoes, passata, chicken stock, peppers and drained chickpeas and stir to combine. Bring the mixture to the boil, then reduce to a simmer and leave to cook for 25 minutes, stirring occasionally.

CAJUN CHICKEN PASTA BAKE

7 Heat the oil in a large pan over a medium heat, then add the onions and garlic and cook for 2–3 minutes, stirring continuously, until soft.
8 Add the tinned tomatoes, passata, chicken stock, frozen peppers and Cajun spice mix and stir to combine. Bring the mixture to the boil, then reduce to a simmer and leave to cook for 25 minutes, stirring occasionally.
9 Meanwhile, cook the pasta in a large pan of boiling water for 8 minutes, until part-cooked. Drain and set aside.
10 When the sauce has finished bubbling, leave to cool slightly then add the drained pasta to the pan and stir to combine. Pour the mixture into a large baking dish and set aside to cool.

CHICKEN, PEPPER & CHICKPEA CURRY CONTINUED...

11 When the sauce has finished bubbling, remove from the heat and stir through the yoghurt. Set aside to cool.

ROAST CHICKEN CONTINUED...

12 The chickens should now be ready to be removed from the oven. Leave to cool slightly, then transfer the birds to a carving board and divide them as below:

- From the first chicken, carve 12 thin slices of breast meat. Remove the 2 chicken legs and pick the meat from the bones, adding it to the pile with the breast meat. This is for your Roast Chicken Dinner.
- Pick the carcass of the first chicken clean, adding the meat to a bowl.
- From the second chicken, carve 8 thin slices of breast meat for the Quesadillas.

- Pick the carcass of the second chicken clean, including the leg meat, shredding the meat and adding to the same bowl as the spare meat from the first chicken. Divide this meat into 2 piles, these will be for the Cajun Chicken Pasta Bake and the Chicken, Pepper & Chickpea Curry.

13 Once cooled, transfer the meat allocated for the Roast Chicken Dinner to a large, labelled freezer bag and freeze flat for up to 3 months.

CHICKEN, PEPPER & CHICKPEA CURRY CONTINUED...

14 Add one of the piles of shredded chicken meat to the cooled curry sauce and stir through. Once cooled to room temperature, transfer to a large, labelled freezer bag and freeze flat for up to 3 months.

CAJUN CHICKEN PASTA BAKE CONTINUED...

15 Add the remaining pile of shredded chicken meat to the dish with the pasta and sauce and stir to combine, then scatter over the shredded mozzarella.

16 Set aside to cool to room temperature, then cover with a lid or a layer of foil, followed by a layer of clingfilm, label and freeze flat for up to 3 months.

CHICKEN, PESTO & MOZZARELLA QUESADILLA WRAPS

17 Set the 4 wraps flat on the counter, then using a pair of scissors cut a straight line from the bottom edge of each wrap to the centre point.

18 Imagining the wraps as 4 quadrants, place 2 slices of chicken breast in the lower left quadrant of each wrap, spread the top left quadrant with a tablespoon of pesto, arrange the chopped cherry tomatoes in the top right quadrant, and put the shredded mozzarella in the bottom right quadrant.

19 Fold the wraps clockwise: bring the bottom left quadrant up and over the top left quadrant, then fold both of those over the top right quadrant, then finally bring everything down over the bottom right quadrant. This should leave you with a neat cone shape.

20 Wrap the folded, filled wraps in foil, then transfer to a large labelled freezer bag and freeze flat for up to 3 months.

WHEN YOU COME TO COOK

ROAST CHICKEN

Remove the roast chicken from the freezer and leave to defrost in the fridge, ideally overnight. Once defrosted, preheat the oven to 180°C/350°F/gas mark 4. Take a large baking sheet and cut a piece of foil double its length. Lay one half of the foil on the baking sheet and arrange your breast slices and leg meat over the top, then fold over the other half of the foil and crimp together the edges to enclose the meat. Reheat in the oven for 10 minutes, until piping hot. Serve the chicken with roast potatoes, your choice of veg, and lots of gravy.

CHICKEN, PEPPER & CHICKPEA CURRY

Remove the curry from the freezer and leave to defrost fully in the fridge, ideally overnight. Once defrosted, tip the curry into a pan over a low heat and cook, stirring occasionally, for 5–10 minutes, until piping hot all the way through. Serve with rice.

CAJUN CHICKEN PASTA BAKE

This can be cooked directly from frozen. Preheat the oven to 180°C/350°F/gas mark 4. Remove the dish from the freezer and remove any clingfilm, then cover the dish in foil and transfer to the oven to bake for 40 minutes. Remove the foil and return to the oven for 20 minutes more, until crisp, golden and piping hot all the way through.

CHICKEN, PESTO & MOZZARELLA QUESADILLA WRAPS

Remove as many quesadilla wraps from the freezer as you need and leave to defrost fully. Once defrosted, remove from the foil and pan-fry in hot, dry pan for 3–4 minutes on each side, until crisp on the outside and piping hot all the way through. These can also be heated on a baking sheet in a 180°C/350°F/gas mark 4 oven for 15 minutes.

Congratulations
You've made 4 meals from 2 chickens!

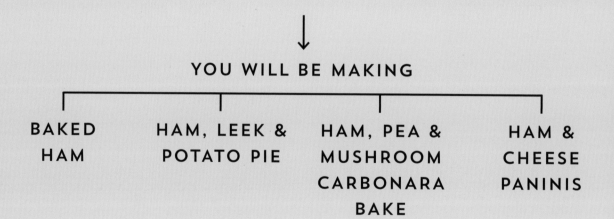

Baked Ham
4 WAYS

↓

YOU WILL BE MAKING

BAKED
HAM

HAM, LEEK &
POTATO PIE

HAM, PEA &
MUSHROOM
CARBONARA
BAKE

HAM &
CHEESE
PANINIS

Adding a packet of sliced ham to your weekly shop is something that many of us do without thinking, but baking your own gives you far more bang for your buck and means that you can use the meat to bulk out delicious family meals and not just for sandwiches! This menu shows you how to take one joint of gammon and turn it into four delicious family meals for the freezer.

Shopping list

Fresh

1.8kg joint boneless gammon

2 large potatoes

1 large leek

1 x 250g block butter

1 litre milk

1 small pot creme fraiche

1 sheet pre-rolled puff pastry

200g white mushrooms

450g pre-grated Cheddar cheese

4 panini rolls

2 beef tomatoes

Frozen

1 x 500g pack frozen chopped onions

1 pack frozen chopped garlic

1 x 800g pack frozen peas

1 x 100g pack frozen chopped parsley (optional)

Storecupboard

1 bottle runny honey

1 jar wholegrain mustard

1 small bottle olive or vegetable oil

1 small bag plain flour

1 pack chicken stock cubes

6 eggs

1 x 500g pack dried pasta (penne or fusilli work well)

1 x 175g pack dried breadcrumbs

1 jar Dijon mustard

INGREDIENTS

BAKED HAM

1.8kg joint boneless gammon

½ cup (140g) runny honey

3 tsp wholegrain mustard

HAM, LEEK & POTATO PIE

2 large potatoes

1 large knob of butter

1 cup (115g) frozen chopped onions

1 large leek

2 tbsp plain flour

generous 1 cup (½ pint) chicken stock

¾ cup (180ml) milk

2 heaped tbsp crème fraîche

1 tbsp frozen chopped parsley

half of the ham chunks
(see step 15 of method)

To cook:

1 sheet pre-rolled puff pastry

1 egg, beaten

HAM, PEA & MUSHROOM CARBONARA BAKE

350g dried pasta
(penne or fusilli work well)

1 tbsp olive or vegetable oil

1 cup (115g) frozen chopped onions

200g sliced mushrooms

2 tsp frozen chopped garlic

1 cup (140g) frozen peas

50g butter

50g plain flour

2 cups (480ml) milk

1 cup (140g) pre-grated Cheddar cheese

half of the ham chunks
(see step 15 of method)

½ cup (23g) breadcrumbs

HAM & CHEESE PANINIS

4 panini rolls

4 slices of baked gammon
(see step 15 of method)

4 handfuls pre-grated Cheddar cheese

Dijon mustard (optional)

2 beef tomatoes, sliced

METHOD

BAKED HAM

1   Preheat the oven to 180°C/350°F/gas mark 4.
2   Put the gammon joint in the base of a large roasting tin, cover with foil and transfer to the oven for 2 hours (or according to packet instructions, if using a different sized joint).
3   When the ham is in the oven, combine the honey and mustard in a bowl and set aside until needed.

HAM, LEEK & POTATO PIE

4   Peel the potatoes and chop into 2.5cm (1 inch) chunks. Put them in a pan, cover with cold water and bring to the boil over a medium heat, then reduce to a simmer and leave to cook for 15–20 minutes, until tender.
5   While the potatoes are cooking, melt the butter in a large, deep-sided frying pan over a medium heat. Add the onions and leek and cook, stirring continuously, for 5 minutes, until soft and translucent.
6   Reduce the heat to low, add the flour and chicken stock to the pan and whisk with the butter, leeks and onions until smooth. Cook for 1 minute, then slowly add the milk, whisking and thickening between each addition, until you have a thick, glossy sauce.
7   Add the crème fraîche to the pan and stir through, then add the parsley and leave to cook, stirring occasionally, for 5 minutes. Remove from the heat and set aside to cool.
8   Once the potatoes are tender, drain through a colander and set aside to cool.

HAM, PEA & MUSHROOM CARBONARA BAKE

9   Cook the pasta in a large pan of boiling water for 8 minutes, until part-cooked. Drain and set aside.
10 Heat the oil in a large, deep-sided frying pan over a medium heat, then add the onions, garlic, mushrooms and frozen peas and cook, stirring continuously, for 6–8 minutes, until the vegetables are tender and the mushrooms have released all of their liquid. Transfer to a bowl and return the pan to the heat.
11 Melt the butter in the same pan over a low heat, then add the flour and mix to a paste. Cook for 1 minute, then slowly add the milk, whisking and thickening between each addition, until you have a thick, glossy sauce. Season with salt and pepper, then remove from the heat.
12 Add the mushroom mixture back to the pan and stir through the sauce, then add the grated Cheddar and stir again.
13 Put the cooled pasta in the base of a large baking dish and pour over the sauce, stirring to fully coat the pasta. Set aside.

BAKED HAM CONTINUED...

14 When the ham has 20 minutes left of its cooking time, remove the foil and pour over the honey and mustard glaze. Return the ham to the oven to cook, uncovered, for its final 20 minutes.

15 When the ham has finished cooking, remove it from the oven and leave to rest for 5 minutes, then transfer to a carving board and divide the joint into:
    • 8 thin slices for the Baked Ham.
    • 4 thin slices for the Ham & Cheese Paninis

• Cut the remaining ham into chunks, making 2 equal piles. These are for the Ham, Leek & Potato Pie and the Ham, Pea & Mushroom Carbonara Bake.

16 Once cooled, transfer the 8 slices of baked ham to a large, labelled freezer bag and freeze flat for up to 3 months.

HAM, LEEK & POTATO PIE CONTINUED...

17 Put the cooled sauce, potatoes and one portion of the ham chunks in a large, labelled freezer bag and give it a mix to combine. Freeze flat for up to 3 months with the sheet of puff pastry alongside so that you can easily grab both from the freezer at the same time.

HAM, PEA & MUSHROOM CARBONARA BAKE CONTINUED...

18 Add the remaining portion of ham chunks to the dish with the pasta and sauce and stir to combine. Sprinkle over the breadcrumbs and set aside to cool to room temperature.

19 Once cooled, cover with a lid or a layer of foil, followed by a layer of clingfilm, label and freeze flat for up to 3 months.

HAM & CHEESE PANINIS

20 Slice the paninis in half, then fill each one with a slice of ham, a handful of cheese and a few slices of tomato. Spread the top halves of the panini rolls with Dijon mustard, if using, then sandwich the paninis and wrap each one in foil. Transfer to a large, labelled freezer bag and freeze flat for up to 3 months.

WHEN YOU COME TO COOK

BAKED HAM

Remove the slices of ham from the freezer and leave to defrost in the fridge, ideally overnight. Once defrosted, preheat the oven to 180°C/350°F/gas mark 4. Take a large baking sheet and cut a piece of foil double its length. Lay one half of the foil on the baking sheet and arrange your ham slices over the top, then fold over the other half of the foil and crimp together the edges to enclose the meat. Reheat in the oven for 10 minutes, until piping hot. Serve the ham with mashed potatoes, your choice of veg, and parsley sauce alongside.

HAM LEEK & POTATO PIE

Remove the pie filling and pastry from the freezer and leave to defrost fully in the fridge, ideally overnight. Once defrosted, preheat the oven to 180°C/350°F/ gas mark 4. Tip the pie filling into a large baking dish and then unroll the pastry sheet over the top. Trim off any excess pastry and press down with a fork all of the way round to seal the pie. Brush the top of the pie with a little of the beaten egg, then transfer to the oven to bake for 30–40 minutes, until the pastry is crisp and golden and the filling is piping hot throughout. Serve hot, with your choice of vegetables alongside.

HAM, PEA & MUSHROOM CARBONARA BAKE

This can be cooked directly from frozen. Preheat the oven to 180°C/350°F/gas mark 4. Remove the dish from the freezer and remove any clingfilm, then cover the dish in foil and transfer to the oven to bake for 1 hour, removing the foil 20 minutes before the end of cooking to allow the top to crisp up, until piping hot all the way through.

CHEESE & HAM PANINIS

Remove the paninis from the freezer and remove the foil. Defrost in the microwave for 2 minutes on the defrost setting, then cook the paninis in a panini press for 4 minutes, until the rolls are crisp and the filling is piping hot.

Congratulations
You've made 4 meals from 1 joint!

Beef Brisket
4 WAYS

↓

YOU WILL BE MAKING

| SLOW COOKED ROAST BRISKET | SMOKY BRISKET CAULIFLOWER CHEESE BAKE | CREAMY BRISKET MUSHROOMS | BRISKET BAGELS WITH CHEESE AND RED ONION |

Beef has a reputation for being expensive, but using a cheaper cut, such as the brisket used here, is a great way to make it a bit more economical. Brisket can be tough, but cooking it low and slow will leave you really juicy, tender meat that will work brilliantly in a range of dishes. This menu shows you how to take one large joint and turn it into 4 delicious family meals for the freezer.

Shopping list

Fresh

1.8kg brisket joint

2 onions

2 large carrots

1 bulb of garlic

1 x 350g bag pre-grated Cheddar cheese

1 red onion

1 large cauliflower

1 x 250g pack butter

568ml (1 pint) milk

300g white mushrooms

300ml double cream

Frozen

1 x 500g pack frozen chopped onions

1 pack frozen chopped garlic

Storecupboard

1 small bottle olive or vegetable oil

1 pack beef stock cubes

1 jar Dijon mustard

4 bagels

1 x 500g pack dried macaroni shells

1 small bag plain flour

1 jar smoked paprika

1 pack dried breadcrumbs

INGREDIENTS

SLOW COOKED ROAST BRISKET

1.8kg brisket joint

2 onions, roughly chopped

2 carrots, roughly chopped

2 tsp frozen chopped garlic

1 tsp Dijon mustard

1 cup (240ml) beef stock

salt and freshly ground black pepper

SMOKY BRISKET CAULIFLOWER CHEESE BAKE

1 cup (140g) dried macaroni shells

1 large cauliflower, cut into florets

60g butter

4 tbsp plain flour

2 cups (480ml) milk

1 tsp smoked paprika

1 cup (140g) pre-grated Cheddar cheese, plus extra for scattering over

half of the brisket chunks (see step 10 of method)

3 tbsp dried breadcrumbs

CREAMY BRISKET MUSHROOMS

1 tbsp olive or vegetable oil

1 cup (115g) frozen chopped onions

2 tsp frozen chopped garlic

300g white mushrooms, sliced

1¼ cups (300ml) double cream

1 tsp Dijon mustard

half of the brisket chunks (see step 10 of method)

salt and freshly ground black pepper

BRISKET BAGELS WITH CHEESE & RED ONION

4 bagels

4 thin slices brisket (see step 10 of method)

4 handfuls pre-grated Cheddar cheese

1 red onion, finely sliced

4 tsp Dijon mustard (optional)

METHOD

SLOW COOKED ROAST BRISKET

1 Preheat the oven to 160°C/320°F/gas mark 3.
2 Put the onions, carrots and garlic in the base of a large roasting tin and stir to combine. Lay the brisket joint over the vegetables and season generously with salt and pepper. Spread the Dijon mustard over the surface of the brisket, then pour the beef stock into the base of the roasting tin.

3 Cover the roasting dish loosely with foil, then transfer the brisket to the oven to cook for 3 hours.
4 Clean down the kitchen sides, then go and do something else until the brisket has 30 minutes left in the oven.

SMOKY BRISKET CAULIFLOWER CHEESE BAKE

5 When the brisket is almost cooked, cook the pasta in a large pan of boiling water for 4 minutes, then add the cauliflower florets to the pan and cook for another 4 minutes. Drain and set aside, keeping the pan on hand for the next stage. (The pasta and cauliflower will be slightly undercooked at this point.)

CREAMY BRISKET MUSHROOMS

6 Heat the oil in a large, deep-sided saucepan over a medium heat, then add the onions, garlic and mushrooms and cook, stirring occasionally, for 6 minutes, until the mushrooms are soft and have released all their liquid.

SMOKY BRISKET CAULIFLOWER CHEESE BAKE CONTINUED...

7 While the mushrooms are cooking, return the pan that you cooked the pasta and cauliflower in to a medium heat and add the butter. Once melted, add the flour and whisk to a paste. Cook for 1 minute, stirring continuously, then slowly pour in the milk, whisking and thickening between each addition, until you have a thick, glossy sauce.
8 Add the paprika, Cheddar cheese and a generous grinding of salt and pepper, and stir to combine.

Stir the part-cooked pasta and cauliflower through the sauce, then set aside until the brisket has finished cooking.

CREAMY BRISKET MUSHROOMS CONTINUED...

9   Once the mushrooms are soft, add the double cream and Dijon mustard to the pan and stir to combine. Cook for 1 minute, stirring continuously, then remove the pan from the heat, season generously, and set aside until the brisket has finished cooking.

SLOW COOKED ROAST BRISKET CONTINUED...

10 The brisket should now be ready to be removed from the oven. Leave to cool slightly, then transfer to a carving board and divide the joint into:
   - 8 thin slices for the Slow Cooked Roast Brisket
   - 4 thin slices for the Brisket Bagels with Cheese and Red Onion
   - Cut the remainder into bite-sized chunks, making a pile each for the Smoky Brisket Cauliflower Cheese Bake and the Creamy Brisket Mushrooms.

11 Once cooled, transfer the 8 slices of brisket for the roast to a large, labelled freezer bag and freeze flat for up to 3 months.

SMOKY BRISKET CAULIFLOWER CHEESE BAKE CONTINUED...

12 Add half of the brisket chunks to the pan with the pasta, cauliflower and cheese sauce and stir to combine.

13 Tip the mixture into a medium baking dish, then scatter over the breadcrumbs and a handful of grated Cheddar cheese.

14 Set aside to cool to room temperature, then cover with a lid or a layer of foil, followed by a layer of clingfilm, label and freeze flat for up to 3 months.

CREAMY BRISKET MUSHROOMS CONTINUED...

15 Add the other half of the brisket chunks to the pan with the mushrooms and stir to combine. Set aside to cool, then transfer to a large, labelled freezer bag and freeze flat for up to 3 months.

BRISKET BAGELS WITH CHEESE & RED ONION

16 Slice the bagels into halves, then place a slice of brisket on the bottom half of each bagel.

17 Scatter a handful of Cheddar over the brisket in each bagel, then top each with some of the sliced onion.

18 Spread the top halves of the bagels with some Dijon mustard, if using, then sandwich the bagels. Wrap each bagel in foil, then transfer them to a large, labelled freezer bag and freeze flat for up to 3 months.

WHEN YOU COME TO COOK

SLOW COOKED ROAST BRISKET

Remove the slices of brisket from the freezer and leave to defrost in the fridge, ideally overnight. Once defrosted, preheat the oven to 180°C/350°F/gas mark 4. Take a large baking sheet and cut a piece of foil double its length. Lay one half of the foil on the baking sheet and arrange your brisket slices over the top, then fold over the other half of the foil and crimp together the edges to enclose the meat. Reheat in the oven for 10 minutes, until piping hot. Serve the brisket with roast potatoes, Yorkshire puddings, your choice of veg, and lots of gravy.

SMOKY BRISKET CAULIFLOWER CHEESE BAKE

This can be cooked directly from frozen. Preheat the oven to 180°C/350°F/gas mark 4. Remove the dish from the freezer and remove any clingfilm, then cover the dish in foil and transfer to the oven to bake for 40 minutes. Remove the foil and return to the oven for 20 minutes more, until crisp, golden and piping hot all the way through.

CREAMY BRISKET MUSHROOMS

Remove the mushrooms from the freezer and leave to defrost fully in the fridge, ideally overnight. Once defrosted, tip the mushrooms into a pan over a low heat and reheat slowly to prevent the sauce from splitting, stirring occasionally, for 5–10 minutes, until piping hot all the way through. Use to dress pasta or spoon over toast.

CHEESY BRISKET BAGELS

Remove as many bagels as you need from the freezer and set aside to defrost. Once defrosted, remove the foil and heat for 1–2 minutes on high in the microwave until the cheese has melted and the bagels are hot all the way through.

Congratulations
You've made 4 meals from 1 joint!

INDEX

ACKNOWLEDGEMENTS

Yay! Another Batch Lady book is out into the world!

There are so many elements to getting a book from the first word written to the bookshelf in your kitchen and it takes a great team to make it happen. My 'batch-it crew', as I fondly call them, are exceptional and I couldn't have put this book together without them.

To my in-house batch-it crew of Nicola Bruce, my sole work mate on a day-to-day basis, thank you for all you do, not only on this book but every day at work. Getting Batch Lady recipes out into the world has required us both to become Jacks of all trades and you attack every task brilliantly. I shall fondly remember the day we cooked through the fish '10 meals in 1 hour' section in my kitchen and laughing at how many cans of tuna and salmon we opened in a day and what we smelled like! It's always great fun working with you, Nicola, and what a fab job you do!

To the batch-it crew at Harper Collins, thank you for continuing to believe in me and my concept. Writing books with HQ has always been so easy and enjoyable that's it's hard to think of it as a job at all – it's always simply fun! So, to Lisa Milton, Kate Fox, Nira Begum, Louise McKeever and the rest of the HQ team, a huge thanks for what you do.

To my batch-it book crew. Firstly, Dan Hurst, my project editor, who has worked with me on every book so far. You do a great job and have always gotten my concepts so well – seeing a book go from reams of single recipes to a finished book is amazing and it's all down to your keen eye and skilled work. You will be very much missed on the batch-it team as you move on to pastures new. To Georgie Hewitt, my designer, who has the hardest job trying to fit my mad ideas for 10 meals in 1 hour onto book pages and find room on the pages for all the freezing and defrosting info, while still making it all look readable and beautiful. As always, another fantastic job, thank you for all you do.

To Cathryn Summerhayes, my agent at Curtis Brown, it's always so great to be asked to write more books and I thank you so much for making this happen.

To photographers Liz Haarala and Max Hamilton. Who would have thought we would still be working with Covid measures when we shot this book?! Budget recipes and freezer recipes are not the easiest to photograph but, as always, you've made them look amazing.

To photographer Ryan Ball, a huge thank you for making me feel so relaxed on your shoots. It was great working with you on the portrait shots for this book.

To my friends, thank you for sticking by me as I take this Batch Lady journey. When busy times hit and I disappear to write, it's lovely to know that when I emerge my friends are still by my side and ready to party as always. A special thanks to my friend Victoria Tweedie who proofread the recipes in this book at every stage. Your eye for detail is brilliant, thank you!

To my wonderful family, Peter you are my rock and always will be. You hold the fort so well when I'm busy on Batch Lady projects and it's so much appreciated. And to Jake and Zara, what amazing young people you have become. Watching you grow into the young adults you are becoming is wonderful and I'm so proud of both of you. Thank you for believing in all I do.

Last, but certainly not least, a huge thank you goes to all of you who follow me online and use my recipes and books. Without you there would be no point to any of this. As we all juggle finances, work-life balance, health, parenting and so much more, it's nice to know that we are in it together and can help each other along. All of you are firmly in my batch-it crew!

Believe in the batch!

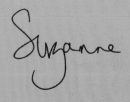